Graphical User Interfaces with Turbo C++

Graphical User Interfaces with Turbo C++

Ted Faison

SAMS

A Division of Macmillan Computer Publishing

11711 North College, Carmel, Indiana 46032 USA

International Standard Book Number: 0-672-22783-5
Library of Congress Catalog Card Number: 90-63191

Acquisitions Editor: *Gregory S. Croy*
Editors: *Robert Ehrgott, Jodi Jensen, and Julia Knispel*
Cover Art and Design: *Dan Armstrong*
Illustrator: *T.R. Emrick*
Indexer: *Sharon Hilgenberg*
Technical Reviewer: *Derrel R. Blain*
Compositor: *Douglas & Gayle, Limited*
Production: *Beth Baker, Betty Kish, Diana Moore, and Joe Ramon*

Printed in the United States of America

Trademarks

To all my girls:
Marilena, Giulia, Claudia, and Linda

Overview

Contents

3   The Screen Handler   **43**

4   Simple Derived Classes   67

9   The Popup Class   161

Preface

This book tells you how to use C++ for building user interfaces. It covers both advanced techniques for general use and specific examples of implementation, but don't expect a tutorial on the C++ language itself. If you are new to C++ but familiar with C, you will still be able to follow the concepts presented, albeit with greater difficulty. I suggest reading a book that deals with C++ programming exclusively before delving into this one.

This book doesn't just describe programming scenarios—it shows you actual source code, with real classes developed to solve real problems. On the companion disk you will also find demo programs that can be executed immediately on any PC-compatible system with EGA graphics. All code and examples shown use the graphics mode exclusively. You can still use the book even if you have no experience with graphics, although you will have some difficulty. The graphics world is alien to many. Even displaying a character on the screen requires operations undefined in the text world. Keep a book on graphics handy, such as one of those listed in the bibliography.

Introduction

In recent years the expression "graphical user interface," or GUI, has gained widespread use. Graphical interfaces differ from traditional interfaces. In a GUI, the user is generally shown some kind of artificial environment, an abstraction of a physical one. Perhaps the most common GUI is the desktop metaphor used by Microsoft Windows and the Apple Macintosh. In such systems the computer displays the basic information-handling objects like those found on or near a real desk: papers, files, file cabinets, and wastebaskets. Using a mouse, the user selects a picture or an icon and either runs a program or initiates a dialog with the system. The expression *graphical user interface* has become a buzzword attached to almost any program that uses a mouse or has a menu system.

Recently GUIs have acquired high-resolution color graphics, shading, and tear-off menus, such as those found on the NeXT computer or under the Open Software Foundation's Motif. These additions provide a more realistic presentation of a physical world created inside the computer. Selections made in dialog boxes are shown in relief, as it were, for a more natural appearance.

This type of interaction with computers has proved to be intuitive, and it can be used by experts and beginners alike. The main user activities involve clicking the mouse and typing commands or text. Observing these activities with a little greater detail, you'll find that the mouse is often used only to initiate operations that require extensive typing, as in word processing or database management.

Limitations of Current GUIs

In an entire class of applications, this simple click-and-type activity does not create a good interface. I refer to these instances as *command-oriented interfaces* (COIs). Consider the scenario of a program used for controlling a petroleum processing plant. The main output to the operator would typically consist of such parameters as temperatures and flow rates. Gauges would represent them—analog gauges for quickly varying parameters and digital gauges for the rest. Pressing buttons and setting parameter levels determine input. Entering alphanumeric data would be extremely rare or even forbidden under such circumstances.

What Is Needed

Many other situations call for similar interface requirements. The controls of a jetliner; musical instruments played remotely via a MIDI interface; monitors and controls of household appliances; and equipment in a radio or television broadcast station: these are just a few such interfaces. The list goes on and on.

Current popular GUIs deal only with traditional programs of word processing, database management, or graphics. The increasing interconnection of computerized systems calls for a single machine capable of synchronizing and orchestrating actions in the overall system. This idea of using computers to control other machines is not new at all. Industrial process-control systems have used computers for this purpose for years.

This book describes a type of GUI designed specifically to use a computer as a control panel. Acting on this panel is equivalent to issuing a command to the machine or program the GUI controls. Traditional GUI features, like dialog windows and scollable text windows, are not developed. You can add them without too much difficulty, following the extensive guidelines given for deriving user classes.

In many cases a COI is convenient to use with a touch-sensitive screen, doing away with the mouse. This allows the user a direct approach in giving commands. Using a touch screen, the user simply touches a displayed object with a finger.

New Concepts Presented

In order to build such an interface, a few new concepts must be introduced. The first impression we want to give a new user is that what appears on the screen represents the control panel of some device. This is referred to as a *control surface*. Because the device being controlled might actually be a program inside the computer, instead of a physical device, it is called a *virtual instrument*. This generalization is important because the user is completely insulated from the details of how commands are carried out.

This level of abstraction also allows a great deal of consistency across a variety of applications. Consistency is essential when building intuitive interfaces. User insulation from implementation details allows the user to develop a mental model of how the system works. The quicker this model is formed, the easier the system will be to the user. This model does not need to correspond to the actual physical one, but it must behave in the same manner. Different users may reason about the interface functionality in different terms or at varying levels of sophistication, but all should be able to feel comfortable with it.

Once the user realizes that the screen is showing a control surface, then everything on the screen is expected to be some kind of control device. Indeed, a typical control surface displays things such as push-buttons, slider potentiometers, gauges, and digital readouts. Only in rare cases is an operator expected to do any typing. A control device is referred to as an *icon*, which is often associated with an object on-screen that is just a label or picture representing a larger entity, such as a program or file. In this book the word *icon* is used extensively to refer to any C++ object involved in the user interface.

In most nontrivial applications, a single control surface is not sufficient or adequate for presenting all the information at hand. Showing too much information can be just as bad as not showing enough. Most people who see a jetliner cockpit are overwhelmed by the number of gauges, knobs, and levers that cover several square meters of surface. In a more rational approach, the pilot calls up on a display device only the parameters that need to be checked, and the system notifies him if something is *not* normal. In fact, the newer jet cockpits are increasingly designed this way. The space shuttle cockpit is equipped for this purpose, with a number of color displays that not only enhance performance but also reliability.

To easily show vast amounts of information in a controlled fashion, the concept of *page* becomes handy. If we organize the control surface as a sequence of pages, as in a book, then we can relegate functions to different pages based on the manner in which they will best be utilized. Thus a control surface will have some kind of page-selecting device, shown directly on the screen with the rest of the controls. With these concepts in mind, I'm ready to define the task to be undertaken in subsequent chapters.

Description of Task

To build a good and complete command-oriented graphical user interface, you have to fit together many different objects: graphical ones, lists of displayed objects, mouse handlers, application programs, event loops, and so on. Later chapters present and describe each of these in detail. This book not only studies the characteristics of GUIs—it shows the actual code required to build a specific program.

At the lowest level of the interface abstraction you find all the boxes, surfaces, buttons, etc. shown on the control surface (the screen). Next comes the organization of these icons into pages; then the package that manages pages, allowing you to flip through them. At the highest level the command dispatcher initiates actions following a user request. The programs described are highly portable, so the source code can be used with any C++ compiler compatible with AT&T release 2.0, with minor changes. Insulation from hardware allows the programs to run on most non-PC-compatible computers with little work. This insulation is achieved by relegating all hardware-dependent features to specific classes, allowing the rest of the system to be completely machine-independent.

Requirements

To compile and run the programs described in this book, you need an IBM PC or AT-compatible computer running DOS V3.1 or higher, equipped with a Microsoft-compatible mouse and an EGA or VGA card.

All code described has been fully tested using three different compilers:

- Turbo C++ Version 1.0

- Borland C++ Version 2.0

- Zortech C++ Version 2.0

You'll find instructions for using the files on this disk in Appendix B, both for Turbo C++ and Zortech users. The companion disk at the back of the book lists the source code for all functions and programs described in this book.

As mentioned, portability allows fast and simple adaptation to different systems and compilers. The programs developed show techniques for writing clean, efficient C++ code that insulates machine dependencies to make porting as easy as possible. At the same time, consideration was given to efficiency issues. Deciding the exact trade-off between optimization and flexibility is always a difficult task and one with which every programmer must eventually deal.

To free the user from compiler-implementation details, several objects have specifically been designed to deal with the graphics display, keyboard, and mouse. Use of direct DOS and BIOS functions has been avoided where possible. To minimize problems, this book uses only those features of the language that will most likely survive in future releases of C++. The language does not have a formal standard, so this is somewhat subjective.

Book Notation

Throughout the book, you need to understand a few conventions in notation and file naming. The following C++ source file naming conventions have been adopted:

- *.cpp (source file)

- *.hpp (header file)

- *.h (standard C++ header file)

- *.prj (TurboC++ project file)

Note that certain compilers use the ANSI C standard suffixes (*.c and *.h) also for C++. This book uses the cpp and hpp suffixes because C++ code does not always compile successfully with an ANSI C compiler, but it's purely a matter of choice.

This book uses the following conventions for such things as functions, macros, variables, and classes:

> Global symbols begin with a capital letter. If a symbol has multiple words, each starts with a capital (for example, RollingBall).Local and private symbols begin with a lower-case letter, and multiple words are separated by an underscore character (for example, rolling_ball).

Macros and #defined symbols are in all capital letters, with multiple words separated by an underscore character (for example, ROLLING_BALL).

Class names are written in italics when they occur in text (for example, *Selector, Potentiometer,* and *Icon).*

Description of Book Chapters

Chapter 1 covers the event handler. It presents advanced techniques for dealing with users via the mouse and the keyboard. The chapter shows a mouse class that is completely reusable and generic.

Chapter 2 discusses how to create a portable graphics object that is fast and reusable. It covers up the rough edges and inconsistencies of the underlying compiler packages, with little run-time speed degradation.

Chapter 3 details the implementation of a *root* class for all displayable objects, showing the power of C++ polymorphism. The chapter's *DisplayList* class is created to manage the objects shown on-screen, and a *Screen* class is discussed to oversee all activity on the user's display device.

Chapter 4 derives the first essential icons, such as boxes, buttons, and cursors, from the base class *Icon*. These objects are considered simple because they are only one or two levels down from the root of the class hierarchy.

Chapter 5 continues the discussion of classes by showing how to build compound objects from simple ones with little additional coding. The chapter describes techniques for building pushbutton banks, potentiometers, and more.

Chapter 6 details the *Page* class, discussing the advantages and disadvantages of the page concept. You will read about typical layouts for pages, and a specific layout is described and implemented.

Chapter 7 gives special emphasis to a single class—*PageSelector*—because page selectors are complicated objects that give a great deal of power. Page selectors manipulate the entire set of pages available through the control surface, so they are almost always needed. They also allow for the rational subdivision of data and command pages for the application.

Chapter 8, perhaps the most interesting chapter, describes objects with the capacity to modify themselves. When you run the demo programs supplied on disk, you will see several practical examples, including bouncing Ping-Pong balls, containers with simulated liquids, and more. You will learn how to create animation on-screen without much code and how to reuse it to make your own animated icons.

A book about user interfaces would be incomplete without Chapter 9, which contains a description of the essential *Popup* class. In this book, popup objects are different from the menus used in Borland's Sidekick or Microsoft Windows. A popup object is a complete-page fragment you can use to "peek" at parts of other pages without switching pages altogether. Chapter 9 discusses the differences between pages and popups and explains the occasions when the latter are pertinent.

Chapter 10 describes how to allow automatic interface-customization saving and restoration each time the program is run. Users often like the option of changing the colors of objects on-screen, and sometimes of even moving them around. Left-handed users can rearrange screen layouts designed for right-handers, making user customizations a permanent part of the program.

Chapter 11 will be most useful for using the objects in this book as a reusable toolbox on which to build and develop more sophisticated or specialized controls. It shows how to use the basic objects to derive new ones that offer customized features.

Chapter 12 discusses the specifics of binding together the user interface with an application. It shows how this step is actually a generic one in most cases because the application can be considered an independent part. The structure of a complete project is described so that the user can understand the control aspects and the flow of information between the application and the interface.

Chapter 13 is a detailed, specific example of how a real project is designed and put together. The chapter points out the necessary decisions regarding page organization. A program developed in the chapter illustrates all the concepts this book presents. With the program you can play music on a displayed piano keyboard. A software recorder enables you to store and play back your melodies.

Chapter 14 underscores the need for portability in an application and touches on the sometimes tough choices a designer faces when considering efficiency and universality. It presents discussions about insulation techniques from compiler, hardware, and operating-system dependencies.

The Event Handler

Events

Some programs are designed to always execute the same way, ignoring the operator once they have begun execution. Such programs might appear to be rather limited because they always produce the same results with a given input, but lots of them are out there. Often these programs are called *filters* because they receive input from somewhere (usually a file), modify the data somehow, and store it somewhere else (usually also in a file). A filter program is started with a given set of parameters and executes until the program is finished. There is essentially no interaction with the user during execution.

One thing that distinguishes a user interface program from a filter is the importance given to the user during execution. What the operator does is very important to the program. In fact, most of the time a user interface program does nothing except wait for the operator to do something. Programmers use the word *event* to refer to something that happens outside a computer that must be detected and processed. In a GUI, the main events are operator actions, such as pressing a key, moving the mouse, or clicking on the mouse. How the GUI responds to an event varies. Some events are considered critical and are handled immediately; others might be queued up for deferred handling; others may be ignored at certain times. One of the main activities of a GUI is to process all these user events.

Detecting Events

The fact that an event has occurred is immaterial to a program unless the event can be detected. Just how this detection occurs is a function of the computer hardware, the importance of the event, its duration, etc. If an event is expected to occur with a certain regularity, a program can periodically check for it at fixed locations in a program. This technique, referred to as *polling*, is both simple and neat but not without problems. There may be a delay, or latency, between the event and its detection because the event is checked only at certain moments. Many events occur at a rate slow enough to be handled by polling, and operator events are often in this category.

On the other side of the spectrum are events that need to be handled as soon as they occur, regardless of what the program is doing at the time. This process requires the event to somehow interrupt the normal program and to force the hardware to redirect its attention to the event. Computers designed to handle events this way have special hardware to allow these interruptions, usually simply called *interrupts*. The entire structure of a program is usually designed to take advantage of interrupts, affecting both the complexity of the program and its timing.

Using Polling

The polling technique is feasible only when an event can be detected during or after its occurrence. Many events leave no trace of themselves, but some do—at least for a while. Consider a serial port receiving characters. If the baud rate is such that characters can be received every millisecond, then checking the port every 100 microseconds will certainly detect a character before it is overwritten.

Polling is also called synchronous detection because the program can detect the events only when it checks for them. Event detection is synchronized with the executing program. Polling is simple, but in large systems it may actually increase the overall complexity. The piece of code that does the polling is contained inside what is called an event loop. Because many large programs check for different events at different times, there can be multiple event loops, with the program switching among them as necessary. A main drawback of polling is the detection latency. With multiple event loops, the timing should be designed so that events are always polled at an adequate rate no matter what is going on in the system.

The GUI described in this book uses the polling technique to detect user commands, and uses a single event loop to keep things as simple as possible.

Using Interrupts

Interrupts are used in all kinds of systems. The PC itself uses interrupts for many internal operations. To support interrupt processing, there must exist a special program, usually called an interrupt service routine (ISR). When an event occurs, an interrupt is triggered, which causes the program being executed to be suspended and the ISR to be executed. When the ISR completes, the old program is resumed where it left off. The code that executes in the absence of interrupts is often called the background process; the ISRs (there may be lots of different ones) are called the foreground processes. The background and foreground processes behave as separate programs executing on the same computer. If the foreground processes execute without leaving any record behind in memory, they cannot interact with the background. Multiple ISRs may interact among themselves and with the background. Processes need to send messages back and forth, or communicate in some fashion in order to work together. All this makes for a more complex program design, but usually leads to superior performance as compared with the polling technique. I won't deal with interrupts here, because I consider it beyond the scope of the book.

The Handler

To deal with events in a consistent way, they are all detected in the event loop that is part of a special object, called the event handler. I use the term handler in this book to refer to an object created once in the GUI and used to control a specific part of the system. Other handlers described later in the book manage the screen and the graphics card.

It might sound reasonable for the GUI to wait for an event and then to call the application program when one is detected. In practice many systems — especially older ones — work in the opposite way. The application program, which has the event loop, calls an I/O function in the interface module when an event needs processing. This haphazard technique lets the application handle I/O however it pleases and opens the door not only to inconsistencies in the interface but also to subtle bugs and duplication of code.

In the GUI description in this book, I enforce a clear separation of roles between the interface and the application program. There is only one event loop, responsible for processing all user events. This loop calls a special event handler to deal with keyboard and mouse activity. To make this event loop technique work correctly, a rule must be followed: application programs are restricted from containing their own event loops and timing loops. The timing through the GUI event loop must remain under control of the GUI at all times. This rule is in contrast with the way some systems work.

Consider, for example, processing a mouse that is moved with a button pressed (a process usually called dragging). If the event handler notifies an object when it is clicked on, that object could conceivably take control for as long as the mouse is being dragged. The problem is that the event handler and the rest of the GUI would be blocked temporarily from execution, and proper system housekeeping would cease. This block would also interfere with the technique used to animate objects. Therefore, the bottom line in this book is that *objects process individual events as appropriate, returning control to the event handler as soon as possible.*

The term *object* is used rather loosely throughout this book, but it generally refers to some kind of entity that consists of both code and data. Most objects are made to be displayed on the screen, and are composed of multiple sub-objects. Figure 1.1 is just an example of an object used to notify the operator.

Fig. 1.1. An object: the OK button in a dialog box.

Keyboard and mouse actions are not the only kinds of events possible in a generic system. A common characteristic of all events is that they represent something which happened in the real world and must be handled somehow. Some events can be handled through the ANSI C *signal()* function. Others may require BIOS or DOS calls. Still others may require writing your own code, with support for interrupts and polling techniques.

This chapter emphasizes *generalization* to restore some order to the growing chaos, and it discusses only the most common events. Events are processed according to their type, and most of them are strongly machine-dependent. The following list shows some types that can be detected:

- Normal keyboard input

- Control-Break input

- Divide-by-zero errors

- Control-C detection

- Keyboard status changes: Shift, Alt, Caps Lock

- Printer errors: not ready, out of paper

- Mouse clicking and dragging

- Software interrupts

- Timer interrupts

- Serial port interrupts

- IEEE 488 bus interrupts

In most systems you don't have to deal with all these events. Often programs deal only with keyboard and mouse input; low-level error handling is a plus. Chapter 14 describes some of the details of DOS error handling.

The useful *System Tick* event is simply a periodic timer interrupt generated by hardware. On PCs and compatibles its rate is 18.2 ticks per second. Although system ticks are easy to generate, they allow software to do many complex operations through scheduling. This book doesn't deal with system ticks as interrupts, but ticks used for certain types of objects are discussed later. (See classes *Delay* and *Clock*.)

Mouse clicks activate the object clicked. Certain objects react to pressing and releasing the mouse buttons. Some allow the mouse to move them around on-screen; others do nothing.

The Input Focus

When you click an object with a mouse, you're really telling the GUI, "give this click command to the object that is under the mouse cursor." That object will receive the event and processes it as necessary. The object that gets commands *has the input focus*.

With mouse commands the user always knows which object has the input focus. This may not be the case when a user is typing on the keyboard. In some systems, the focus belongs to the object on which you place the mouse cursor, regardless of clicking. It is entirely up to the object itself to handle the keypress.

Any object with the input focus must be able to consume the event it receives. This process of consummation involves removing the event from the system so that it won't be processed more than once. For example, a keystroke event requires removing a character from the keyboard buffer. In some systems a queue stores events. The event then must be removed from the queue when it is processed.

Inside Class Events

This class handles system events and user input, often dealing with low-level functions that use direct DOS calls. Because such calls are not standardized in C++ implementations, the entire class tends to depend on the type of machine used. This book relegates *all* machine-dependent functions to the classes *Events* and *Graphics*. The former deals with inputs and general event handling, the latter with screen output. To port the GUI to another compiler or machine would require modifying only two classes. The following list shows the kinds of events handled by class *Events*:

- Mouse activity

- Programmable delays

- Keyboard activity

- System timer functions

- Sound functions

- Interrupt control

Subclasses handled through *Events* realize some of these features; member functions in the class realize others. This book, by stressing ANSI C compatible functions, leaves only two differences between Turbo C++ and Zortech C++ implementations. Renaming the two functions *enable()* and *disable()* in the class header file resolves the problems easily. These functions, which deal with the hardware interrupts, are not standardized in C. An alternative to using the C functions is to call two assembly language routines. This strategy solves the compiler incompatibility problem, but the routines still won't be portable to non-8086 machines.

The Mouse Class

In any system there is going to be machine-dependent code. A good design segregates this code into a single module so that porting to a different machine has the least impact possible on the rest of the system (hopefully none). The event handler is responsible for handling all input events, which includes mouse activity. Obviously the mouse is a physical object that must be realized in its own class, but I have designed the event handler so that it alone has access to the mouse. For this reason the class *Mouse* can be considered a subclass on the class *Events*.

Restricting access to an entire class is a powerful construct: it prevents unauthorized use and enforces consistency.

Most compilers provide no support for the increasingly popular mouse, which still isn't considered standard equipment on PCs and compatibles. However, Borland has added mouse support to Turbo C++ in its Programmer's Platform interface. Turbo C++ itself does not support the mouse. Zortech C++ *does* support it through a "mouse package"—functions written in traditional C style.

A new *Mouse* class is one way to make the most common mouse functions available to any standard DOS C++ compiler. This book uses a mouse-compatible class written to support Microsoft mice. MSC Technologies, Inc., and Logitech both manufacture Microsoft-compatible mice, and together the three make up the bulk of installed mice for PCs.

Microsoft introduced its first mouse several years ago, and the driver has continued to evolve. Some early mouse functions such as the lightpen are either obsolete or practically useless. This book doesn't deal with the lightpen. If you need a function not included in here, you can easily add it to the class by following the guidelines given.

The rendezvous point between the mouse driver and the GUI is 8086 software interrupt 0x33, selected by Microsoft. All mouse functions vector through this interrupt. The Microsoft driver's so-called "internal flag" syndrome irritates many computer users. This internal flag, a counter used by the driver, indicates the status of the mouse cursor. Its value is not available outside the driver. Issuing a MOUSE_SHOW function call increments the flag, and a MOUSE_HIDE call decrements the call. Unfortunately, calling the MOUSE_SHOW function *n* times requires you to call MOUSE_HIDE *n* times to remove the cursor. The *Mouse* class solves this problem by encapsulating a mouse status variable that tracks the intentions of the application. If by mistake you call *Mouse::Show* twice, one call to *Mouse::Hide* is sufficient to erase it.

Class *Mouse* solves another Microsoft driver problem, the screen coordinate system. Some systems, such as the Borland Graphics Interface (BGI) and the Microsoft mouse driver, assign the origin to the upper left corner. Yet the Zortech flash graphics package assigns it to the lower left corner.

All the GUI examples in this book follow the right-handed Cartesian system, universally used in analytical geometry and calculus. The Cartesian system places the screen origin in the lower left corner. The X axis is the horizontal axis, the Y axis the vertical one. All coordinates given to and returned from class *Mouse* will use this convention, allowing the graphics and mouse functions to work in the same coordinate system.

Using a class approach to the mouse simplifies the code. With the Zortech compiler, you have to call the mouse function *msm_init()* before using the mouse and *msm_term()* before exiting to DOS. Class *Mouse* requires only that you define an object of class *Mouse*, with its scope the same as or wider than the application program. The constructor automatically performs the initialization (calling the driver to initialize itself and hide the mouse cursor), and the destructor performs the cleanup (calling the driver to deactivate itself and remove the mouse cursor from the screen).

The Virtual Coordinate System

Many people have trouble when initially programming the mouse because of the confusing coordinate system used by the mouse driver. Users expect the mouse position to be in terms of pixels, when in fact this is not always the case. The mouse driver uses a special virtual coordinate system to aid in dealing with different display adaptors. Most of the trouble occurs with CGA display adaptors because the mouse always reports its location using a virtual coordinate system, which may not correspond to the actual screen resolution. Luckily this is not true for EGA and VGA adaptors. This virtual system, intended to provide a degree of insulation from the display adaptor being used, can cause a little difficulty. The code in this book does *not* support CGA adaptors, so the mouse coordinate system has the same resolution as the screen.

The screen resolution of PCs and compatibles depends on the display adapter and the screen mode. The former is a hardware choice, the latter a software one. The initialization of the *Graphics* object (described in Chapter 2) selects a 640 x 350 pixel screen mode, available on both EGA and VGA adapters. The mouse uses the same virtual coordinate system. Otherwise, the necessary conversions between systems would have to come from class *Mouse*. Listing 1.1 shows the header for class *Mouse*.

Listing 1.1. The header file for class Mouse.

```
#ifndef MOUSEHPP
#define MOUSEHPP

#include <dos.h>
#include <stdlib.h>

#include "graphics.hpp"

#define MOUSE_INTERRUPT 0x33

// mouse buttons definitions
#define MOUSE_LEFT_BUTTON      1
#define MOUSE_RIGHT_BUTTON     2

enum DisplayMode {
  MOUSE_OFF = -1,
  MOUSE_ON = 0
};

// define the mouse driver command code in terms
// of the Microsoft Mouse function number
enum MouseFunctionCode {
    MOUSE_RESET = 0,
    MOUSE_SHOW,
    MOUSE_HIDE,
    MOUSE_STATUS,
    MOUSE_SET_POSITION,
    MOUSE_PRESSED_INFO,
    MOUSE_RELEASED_INFO,
    MOUSE_X_RANGE,
    MOUSE_Y_RANGE
};
```

Listing 1.1 Continues

Listing 1.1 Continued

```
class Mouse {

    REGS results;
    DisplayMode display_status;
    int RightHandedCartesian(int);
    void ButtonInfo(MouseFunctionCode, int, int*,
                int*, int*, int*);
    int MouseCommand(MouseFunctionCode,
                unsigned int bx = 0,
                unsigned int cx = 0,
                unsigned int dx = 0);
public:

    Mouse();
    void Show();
    void Hide();
    int Status(int*, int*);
    void SetPosition(int, int);
    void ButtonPressedInfo(int, int*, int*,
                        int*, int*);
    void ButtonReleasedInfo(int, int*, int*,
                        int*, int*);
    void SetXRange(int, int);
    void SetYRange(int, int);

    int LeftButtonDown();
    int RightButtonDown();
    int BothButtonsDown();

    ~Mouse() {}
};

#endif
```

In the header file, the macros MOUSE_LEFT_BUTTON and MOUSE_RIGHT_BUTTON were defined to insulate the user and the Mouse class from idiosyncrasies of mouse implementations. Drivers from the various mouse manufacturers don't all have a common convention for numbering the mouse buttons. Even the Microsoft driver itself is inconsistent in the way it handles the buttons. For example, with the command *Mouse::Mouse(MOUSE_STATUS)* the driver returns a 1 for the left button and a 2 for the right one. Inside the function *Mouse::ButtonInfo(...)* the mouse driver expects a 0 for the left button and a 1 for the right. The *Mouse* class is more consistent, and uses a uniform set of values for the mouse buttons.

The *enum MouseFunctionCode* lists the mouse-driver function codes supported by the *Mouse* class. Using an *enum* allows the compiler to type-check the commands passed among the *Mouse* member functions. Listing 1.2 shows the code for class *Mouse*.

Listing 1.2. The implementation of class Mouse.

```cpp
#include "mouse.hpp"

Mouse::Mouse()
{
    display_status = MOUSE_OFF;

    // terminate program if no mouse installed
    if (MouseCommand(MOUSE_RESET) == 0) {
      GraphicsHandler->PutString(BRIGHT_RED,
        100, 100, "Mouse driver not installed.");
      exit(1);
    }
}

void Mouse::Show()
{
    if (display_status == MOUSE_ON)
      return;
    display_status = MOUSE_ON;
    MouseCommand(MOUSE_SHOW);
}

void Mouse::Hide()
{

    if (display_status == MOUSE_OFF)
      return;
    display_status = MOUSE_OFF;
    MouseCommand(MOUSE_HIDE);
}

int Mouse::Status(int* x, int* y)
{
    // read the button and (X, Y) status
    MouseCommand(MOUSE_STATUS);

    // save the X coordinate of the mouse
    *x = results. x. cx;

    // save the Y coordinate of the mouse,
    // after converting to a right-handed
    // coordinate system, in which the lower left
    // corner of the screen is the origin
    *y = RightHandedCartesian(results. x. dx);

    // return the button status
    return results. x. bx;
}
```

Listing 1.2 Continues

Listing 1.2 Continued

```
int Mouse::MouseCommand(MouseFunctionCode function,
                 unsigned int bx,
                 unsigned int cx,
                 unsigned dx)
{
     REGS command;

     command. x. ax = function;
     command. x. bx = bx;
     command. x. cx = cx;
     command. x. dx = dx;
     int86(MOUSE_INTERRUPT, &command, &results);
     return results. x. ax;
}


void Mouse::SetPosition(int x, int y)
{
     // convert screen coordinates to a right
     // handed system
     y = RightHandedCartesian(y);
     MouseCommand(MOUSE_SET_POSITION, 0, x, y);
}

void Mouse::ButtonPressedInfo(int button,
                 int* status,
                 int* count,
                 int* x,
                 int* y)
{
     ButtonInfo(MOUSE_PRESSED_INFO,
           button, status, count, x, y);
}

void Mouse::ButtonReleasedInfo(int button,
                 int* status,
                 int* count,
                 int* x,
                 int* y)
{
     ButtonInfo(MOUSE_RELEASED_INFO,
           button, status, count, x, y);
}

void Mouse::ButtonInfo(MouseFunctionCode command,
                 int button,
                 int* status,
                 int* count,
                 int* x,
                 int* y)

{
```

```
        if ( (button == MOUSE_LEFT_BUTTON) ||
             (button == MOUSE_RIGHT_BUTTON) )

            // convert to Microsoft format
            button--;

        else {
          // invalid button parameter: clear variables
          *status = 0;
          *count = 0;
          *x = 0;
          *y = 0;
          return;
        }

        *status = MouseCommand(command, button);
        *count = results. x. bx;
        *x = results. x. cx;
        *y = RightHandedCartesian(results. x. dx);
}

void Mouse::SetXRange(int x1, int x2)
{
        MouseCommand(MOUSE_X_RANGE, 0, x1, x2);
}

void Mouse::SetYRange(int y1, int y2)
{
        MouseCommand(MOUSE_Y_RANGE, 0,
                RightHandedCartesian(y1),
                RightHandedCartesian(y2) );
}


int Mouse::LeftButtonDown()
{
        int x, y;
        return (Status(&x, &y) & MOUSE_LEFT_BUTTON) ?
            TRUE : FALSE;
}

int Mouse::RightButtonDown()
{
        int x, y;
        return (Status(&x, &y) & MOUSE_RIGHT_BUTTON) ?
            TRUE : FALSE;
}


int Mouse::BothButtonsDown()
{
```

Listing 1.2 Continues

Listing 1.2 Continued

```
                    return LeftButtonDown() && RightButtonDown();
        }


        int Mouse::RightHandedCartesian(int y)
        {
                    return GraphicsHandler->ScreenHeight() - y;
        }
```

Function Descriptions

Mouse::Mouse

The class constructor sets its private copy of the mouse driver's *internal display flag* to the initial value, and then it attempts to initialize the driver. If all goes well, the function returns; otherwise, an error message is displayed, and the entire program is aborted. This might not be acceptable for some systems if the presence of the mouse is optional. In this book a mouse is necessary. If the driver initializes correctly, the mouse is left undisplayed, as indicated by the value of *display_status*.

Mouse::Show

This function displays the mouse cursor at its current position. After initialization the cursor goes undisplayed to the middle of the screen. This function prevents multiple invocations of the MOUSE_SHOW function of the mouse driver without intervening calls to MOUSE_HIDE, which in turn prevents the "internal flag" problem.

Mouse::Hide

This is the counterpart of Show. The cursor is removed from the display, but its coordinates are not modified. Requesting the mouse status returns correct coordinates regardless of whether the mouse is visible.

Mouse::Status

This is the most commonly used mouse function in this book. It returns a bit mask of the mouse buttons pressed plus the instantaneous mouse coordinates, using the standard right-handed coordinate system.

Mouse::MouseCommand

This private function is the interface between the *Mouse* class and the mouse driver. It handles the low-level details of register values and DOS interrupts. Notice how the function's parameters assume default values of zero if not used. This assumption allows a single function to handle all the mouse driver functions. DOS interrupt 0x33 invokes these driver functions, which require loading the 8086 registers with values that depend on the service requested. In general the `ax` register always contains the function code identifying this service. The *enum* MouseFunctionCode defines the function codes this book has implemented. Some functions use the `bx` register to indicate which mouse button you have pressed or released. The `cx` and `dx` registers sometimes have x and y coordinate values (using the native mouse coordinate system). To make matters more complex, not all the driver functions use the registers. Consult the Microsoft mouse driver specifications for further information. MouseCommand hides all this mess and provides a single, clean interface to the mouse driver. Better yet, you need no assembly language, although there is some very machine-dependent code.

Mouse::SetPosition

This function sets the mouse cursor location at the given location. Note that the cursor occupies several pixels, but its *hot point* defines its position. The standard mouse cursor's hot point is the tip of the left-pointing arrow. Setting the position outside of valid X and Y boundaries (see the functions SetXRange and SetYRange that follow) defaults the position to the closest point inside those boundaries. For example, assume the coordinates 300 and 500 on the X axis and 200 and 400 on the Y axis constrain the mouse. Attempting to set the mouse position at (0, 0) causes it to go to (300, 200).

Mouse::ButtonPressedInfo

This member function returns the following data regarding a selected button (only one button can be handled at a time):

status   Whether the button is up or down

count   The number of times the button was pressed since the last call to this function

x, y   The coordinates of the mouse the last time the button was pressed

Mouse::ButtonReleasedInfo

This member function is the counterpart of the preceding one. It returns the following data regarding a selected button:

status   Whether the button is up or down

count   The number of times the button was released since the last call to this function

x, y   The coordinates of the mouse the last time the button was released

Mouse::ButtonInfo

This private function handles the details for the preceding two. It type checks the mouse-button argument and converts it to the Microsoft format. Then the driver is invoked, and the (x, y) coordinates returned are converted to the standard right-handed system.

Mouse::SetXRange

This function sets the boundaries of the mouse cursor's movement along the X axis. After initialization, the boundaries are set to the size of the virtual mouse coordinate system.

The values used for the X limits are not range-checked. Using values less then 0 for the lower limit allows the mouse cursor to travel off the left side of screen, because the mouse driver allows it to go all the way to –32768. The upper limit likewise can reach a value beyond 640, the normal screen size. You can go as high as 32767, and the mouse can then run far off the right side of the screen. If you run into trouble by erroneously setting the X range to absurd values, then you might want to consider range-checking the x1 and x2 parameters before using them.

Mouse::SetYRange

This function works like the preceding one but affects the Y axis. Notice the coordinate system conversion of the coordinates.

Mouse::LeftButtonDown

This function simply returns a true/false value based on the instantaneous status of the left mouse button at the time of the function call.

Mouse::RightButtonDown

This function is the counterpart for the preceding function, but it deals with the right mouse button.

Mouse::BothButtonsDown

This function combines the features of the preceding two functions.

Mouse:: RightHandedCartesian

This useful short function converts a left-handed coordinate system into a right-handed one. All that's involved is an inversion of the Y axis so that it increases upward.

Mouse Interrupt Artifacts

Running some of the demo programs on some systems might reveal that moving the mouse sometimes disturbs certain objects. Chapter 8 deals with these objects, which can update themselves on the screen when necessary. Moving the mouse generates an interrupt, and the mouse cursor disappears and then reappears at a new position on the screen. When the mouse tries to move its cursor while objects are being painted on the screen, the conflict in the commands reaches the graphics card: the object is trying to paint itself and so is the mouse. Simultaneous commands from two unrelated sources—the mouse driver and the GUI—can both hit the display adapter while the screen is being written to. Here are two possible solutions:

1. Check the version of the mouse driver installed. Is it available in a version that handles EGA and VGA cards correctly? Mouse Systems, Inc., offers its mouse-driver version 6.22, which works capably in many systems.

2. Disable any interrupts inside animated objects just before they modify the screen; then restore the interrupts.

The second solution allows any mouse driver and display adapter combination to work together. The first solution is not available to owners of old mouse drivers with display adapters not 100 percent compatible with them.

The Delay Class

Most systems need software programmable delays, regardless of how slow the machine seems compared to the software. Even a simple program to issue a "beep" sound needs the speaker turned on awhile. Here you need a software delay function. It contains a loop that executes in a given amount of time. This is not a good generic solution because the speed of the computer hardware conditions the time of execution of the delay loop.

It's better to use the PC's hardware timer chip to *find* how fast the computer is and to calibrate the delay function to this speed. Turbo C++'s *delay* function serves this purpose, but it is not standard in C++. One solution is a new class to be used with any C++ compiler that supports DOS calls via 8086 software interrupts. The *Delay* class implements this function and hides all the details from the user. It provides a machine-independent *Wait* function whose argument is in milliseconds (mS). Listings 1.3 and 1.4 show the files the class uses.

Listing 1.3. The header file for class Delay.

```
#ifndef DELAYHPP
#define DELAYHPP

#include <dos.h>

#define READ_BIOS_TICK_COUNT 0
#define GET_BIOS_TICK_COUNT_INTERRUPT 0x1A

class Delay {

    long one_millisecond;
    void DelayOneMillisecond();
    long DosTickCount();

public:

    Delay();
    void Wait(long milliseconds);
};

#endif
```

Listing 1.4. The implementation of class Delay.

```
#include "delay.hpp"

Delay::Delay()
{
    // calibrate the delay object according
    // to the speed of the computer

    // wait for a system tick
    long count = DosTickCount();
    while (count == DosTickCount() )
        ;
    count = DosTickCount();

    // count until the next tick
```

Listing 1.4 Continues

Listing 1.4 Continued

```
          long delay;
          for (delay = 0; ; delay++)
            if (count != DosTickCount() ) break;

          // save the count
          one_millisecond = delay / 2;
      }

      void Delay::Wait(long delay)
      {
          for (long time = 0; time < delay; time++)
            DelayOneMillisecond();
      }


      void Delay::DelayOneMillisecond()
      {
          for (int i = 0; i < one_millisecond; i++)
            ;
      }

      long Delay::DosTickCount()
      {
          REGS command, results;
          long time;

          command. x. ax = READ_BIOS_TICK_COUNT;
          int86(GET_BIOS_TICK_COUNT_INTERRUPT,
                &command, &results);
          time = results. x. cx;
          return  (time << 16) + results. x. dx;
      }
```

Function Descriptions

Delay::Delay

The class constructor determines the speed of the hardware, setting the value of the machine-dependent variable ***delay***. DOS maintains a counter that is incremented at every system tick, about 18.2 times a second. The constructor first synchronizes itself with the system tick, then executes a loop to determine how many times it can run before the next system tick. After the loop count is determined, it is divided by 2 and stored. This value is subsequently used as a loop counter so that function *Delay::DelayOneMillisecond()* executes in about one millisecond, regardless of the speed of the PC on which it executes.

Delay::Wait

This function takes an argument, assumed to be in milliseconds. The function returns only after the requested time has passed.

Delay::DelayOneMillisecond

This private function is the heart of the *Delay* class. It is a simple loop that takes 1 millisecond to execute, regardless of whether it is run on a PC, a 286 AT, or a 386 AT.

Delay::DosTickCount

This private function invokes the ROM BIOS to read the current system tick count. DOS increments this value with every tick and shows it as a 32-bit value. The function is used by the class constructor to calibrate the function *DelayOneMillisecond* to the hardware speed.

The Header File for the Events Class

Now that you've studied the major component classes of *Events*, you need to look at the header file for the class. The header file insulates the rest of the GUI from most machine dependencies. Some functions deal with input events, such as mouse and keyboard activity. Some deal with machine-dependent and output events, such as sound generation and delays. The degree of compiler independence provided by class *Events* is considerable. The only change necessary with the Zortech compiler is renaming the two interrupt handling functions. Using conditional compilation directives in the header file performs this change. When you use the Zortech compiler, you should define the macro ZORTECH in the file *constant.hpp* before compiling the *Events* class.

Next comes a series of strictly PC-dependent definitions, mostly regarding use of the timer chip. Inside the class are two private objects, *mouse* and *delay*. Merely declaring them makes them initialize automatically when you create an object of class *Events*.

The mouse-interface functions, declared inline, use the separate *Mouse* class. All mouse commands must pass through the *Events* class interface.

Next come the keyboard functions, which provide insulation from BIOS calls. The *Wait* member function uses the *Delay* class to provide machine-independent delays. The next sound functions use the timer chip to issue sound through the timer chip. The last two inline functions use the Turbo C++ interrupt functions to control the 80x86 interrupts. Listings 1.5 and 1.6 show the complete listings of the *Events* class files.

Listing 1.5. The header file for class Events.

```
#ifndef EVENTSHPP
#define EVENTSHPP

#include <bios.h>
#include <stdio.h>
#include <stdlib.h>
#include <time.h>
#include <dos.h>

#include "mouse.hpp"
#include "icon.hpp"
#include "screen.hpp"
#include "graphics.hpp"
#include "constant.hpp"
#include "database.hpp"
#include "delay.hpp"

#if ZORTECH
#include <int.h>
#define enable() int_on()
#define disable() int_off()
#endif

// setup some IBM PC constants

// the PC's timer chip frequency in Hz
#define TIMER_CLOCK            1193280

// timer chip commands and ports
#define TIMER_SET_COMMAND      0xB6
#define TIMER_COMMAND_PORT     0x43
#define TIMER_DATA_PORT   0x42
#define TIMER_CONTROL_PORT     0x61

// standard frequencies and delays
#define ONE_KILOHERTZ          1000
#define BEEPER_DELAY           30

class Events {

        Mouse mouse;
```

```
        Delay delay;

public:

        Events();

        // mouse functions
        void ShowMouseCursor() {mouse. Show(); }
        void HideMouseCursor() {mouse. Hide(); }
        void ProcessMouseActions();

        // keyboard functions
        int GetKeyPressed();
        int AnyKeysPressed();
        void ProcessUserKeys();

        // DOS time functions
        long SystemTime();
        char* CurrentTime(float = 0);

        void Wait(long period) {delay. Wait(period);}

        // sound functions
        void Beep();
        void SoundOn(int frequency = ONE_KILOHERTZ,
                   unsigned int duration = 0);
        void SoundOff();

        void DisableInterrupts() {disable(); }
        void EnableInterrupts() {enable(); }
};

extern Events* EventsHandler;

#endif
```

Listing 1.6. The implementation of class Events.

```
#include "events.hpp"

Events::Events()
    {
        // initialize the coodinates of the string
        // editing insertion point
        InsertionBarX = UNDEFINED_COORDINATE;
        InsertionBarY = UNDEFINED_COORDINATE;
    }


    int Events::GetKeyPressed()
    {
```

Listing 1.6 Continues

Listing 1.6 Continued

```cpp
        // wait until a key is pressed, then
        // return its value
        return bioskey(0);
}

int Events::AnyKeysPressed()
{
        // return zero if no keys are ready to
        // be read from the keyboard
        return bioskey(1);
}

void Events::ProcessUserKeys()
{
        // see if any keys are pressed
        if (AnyKeysPressed() ) {

          // read the next key
          int key = GetKeyPressed();

          // see if there is an icon that has the
          // keyboard focus
          if (InsertionBarX == UNDEFINED_COORDINATE) return;
          if (InsertionBarY == UNDEFINED_COORDINATE) return;

          // turn off the mouse cursor before processing
          // the keypress
          mouse. Hide();

          // let the icon with the input focus process
          // the key
          CurrentScreen->KeyTyped(InsertionBarX,
                                  InsertionBarY, key);

          // restore the mouse cursor
          mouse. Show();
        }
}

void Events::ProcessMouseActions()
{
        static int old_x, old_y;
        static status, old_status;
        static Icon* current_icon;
        int x, y, changes;

        // save the status of the mouse buttons that
        // were processed previously
        old_status = status;

        // get the current mouse button status
        status = mouse. Status(&x, &y);
```

```
    /* see if mouse was moved with a button pressed
    if (current_icon) {
      if ( (x != old_x) || (y != old_y) ) {
        if (mouse. LeftButtonDown() )
          // it was: let the icon process the event
          current_icon->LeftButtonDragged(x - old_x,
                              y - old_y,
                              status);
      }
    }

    /* update the mouse coordinates for next time around
    old_x = x;   old_y = y;

    if (status == old_status)
      // no new mouse events to process yet
      return;

    // record the change from last time around
    changes = status ^ old_status;

    if (changes & MOUSE_LEFT_BUTTON) {
      // the left mouse button was pressed
      // turn off the mouse cursor before processing
      mouse. Hide();

      // save the icon that was clicked on, in case
      // the mouse is dragged on it
      current_icon = CurrentScreen->CurrentIcon(x, y);

      // process the mouse button click
      CurrentScreen->LeftButtonChanged(x, y, status);

      // restore the mouse cursor
      mouse. Show();
    }

    // terminate the program when the RIGHT mouse
    // button is clicked anywhere on the screen
    if (changes & MOUSE_RIGHT_BUTTON) {
      GraphicsHandler->Terminate();
      exit(0);
    }
}

long Events::SystemTime()
{
    time_t system_time;
    // read the system time, showing the number
    // of seconds elapsed since 1/1/70
    time(&system_time);
```

Listing 1.6 Continues

25

Listing 1.6 Continued

```
        return (long) system_time;
    }

char* Events::CurrentTime(float time_difference)
{
    // get the current time
    long the_time = SystemTime();

    // adjust system time for the difference
    // between time zones
    the_time += time_difference * 3600;

    // convert to the ANSI standard string format:
    // WWW MMM DD hh:mm:ss YYYY\n
    // for example, "WED JAN 15 14:52:29 1990\n"
    char* string = ctime(&the_time);

    // skip to the hour field, and truncate the
year
    string += 11;
    *(string + 8) = '\0';
    return string;
}

void Events::Beep()
{
    // issue a short sound at 1000Hz
    SoundOn(ONE_KILOHERTZ, BEEPER_DELAY);
}

void Events::SoundOn(int frequency, unsigned
duration)
{
    // ignore invalid frequencies
    if (frequency == 0) return;

    // compute IBM PC timer value
    int timer_value = TIMER_CLOCK / frequency;

    // program hardware timer's frequency
    outp(TIMER_COMMAND_PORT, TIMER_SET_COMMAND);
    outp(TIMER_DATA_PORT, timer_value & 0xff);
    outp(TIMER_DATA_PORT, timer_value >> 8);

    // turn on the speaker, preserving unused bits
    int old = inp(TIMER_CONTROL_PORT);
    outp(TIMER_CONTROL_PORT, old | 3);

    // keep it on for the time specified, or
```

```
indefinitely
    if (duration == 0) return;
    Wait(duration);
    SoundOff();
}

void Events::SoundOff()
{
    // turn off the speaker, preserving unused
bits
    int old = inp(TIMER_CONTROL_PORT);
    outp(TIMER_CONTROL_PORT, old & 0xFC);
}
```

Function Descriptions

Events::Events

This constructor is invoked whenever you create an event handler. Only one such handler is expected to be present in the GUI shown here, but a multiuser system might define a separate event handler for each operator terminal. The C++ compiler then also calls the constructors for the private objects *mouse* and *delay* declared in the header file. The function also initializes the coordinates of the *insertion bar*, which holds the coordinates of the object with the input focus for keyboard events. A key typed on the keyboard is sent to the object holding the input focus, if any.

Events::GetKeyPressed

This function calls BIOS and waits for the user to press a key on the keyboard before returning its value. If keys had been pressed before calling *GetKeyPressed*, the function would get the first one from the keyboard buffer maintained by DOS and return immediately.

Events::AnyKeysPressed

This function checks to see whether any keys are available for processing.

Events::ProcessUserKeys

This function checks to see if the user pressed any keys on the keyboard. If so, it reads the key and passes it along to be processed by the icon that currently has the input focus, i.e., the last icon you clicked on. As explained at the beginning of this chapter, only one icon at a time can receive the characters typed by the user; this object has the system's "input focus." You give the input focus to an object by clicking on it. Note that none of the objects described in this book processes keystrokes. If you wish to add this capability, you'll need to add appropriate code to the function *KeyTyped()* described in chapter 3.

Events::ShowMouseCursor

This function merely invokes the corresponding function in the private *Mouse* subclass to display the mouse cursor on the screen. The cursor is shown as an arrow pointing upward and to the left. The is the default cursor provided by the Microsoft mouse driver when operating in the 640 x 350 graphics mode.

Events::HideMouseCursor

This function removes the mouse cursor from the display. The purpose of the function is to allow generic objects access to the Hide function of the private *Mouse* subclass.

Events::ProcessMouseActions

This function handles all the events the mouse can generate. These include clicking the left or right buttons and moving the mouse while you hold one of the mouse buttons (dragging the mouse).

Dragging the mouse on an icon invokes that icon's LeftButtonDragged function. Pressing or releasing the mouse's left button passes the event to the Screen handler, which will be described in chapter 3.

Use the right mouse button for only one purpose in this book: terminating the program. An actual system would probably use the button for something more interesting.

Events::SystemTime

This function uses the ANSI function *time()* to read the system time. The return value indicates the number of seconds elapsed since January 1, 1970. Function *Events::SystemTime ()* takes this value and casts it into a long integer.

Events::CurrentTime

This function reads the system time and date, adjusts it for the indicated time zone, which defaults to the local one, converts it to string format, and then returns a pointer to it. Note that the a static buffer declared in *ctime* stores the string itself and that each call overwrites it.

Events::Beep

This function issues a short beep using the PC speaker, which lasts 30 milliseconds at 1000 Hz.

Events::SoundOn

This function uses the PC timer chip to issue a square wave through the system speaker. The sound level of the signal is not adjustable directly. The default parameters generate a 1KHz signal issued for an indefinite time. Function *Events::SoundOn(...)* converts the sound frequency into an internal value used by the timer chip. When a command is issued to this chip, only the bits connected to the timer chip are modified. If *Events::SoundOn(...)* is called with a null duration parameter, the function turns the speaker on and exits immediately.

Events::SoundOff

This function just turns the speaker off. It deactivates but does not restore the sound chip to its previous state, because class *Events* has no idea what the chip's state was. It has no way of finding out, either, because the timer-chip port is write-only. A solution could be using a separate *TimerChip* class to control the chip with its own record of the values sent to the port. All access to the chip would occur through this class, so data would always be available on the current setting of the chip.

Events::DisableInterrupts

This function disables hardware interrupts by invoking the TurboC++ function *disable()*. When compiling the *Events* class with the ZORTECH macro defined in the *constant.hpp* file, the function invoked will be the Zortech equivalent function *int_off()*.

Events::EnableInterrupts

This is the counterpart for the previous function. It invokes the Turbo C++ function *enable()* to allow processing of hardware interupts. When compiling the *Events* class with the ZORTECH macro defined in the *constant.hpp* file, the function invoked is the Zortech equivalent function *int_on()*.

2

The Graphics Handler

Is it possible to build a graphical user interface without graphics? Yes and no. The answer depends on what you consider *graphics* to be. Many systems claim to be graphically oriented only because they use pull-down menus with character boxes and lines. Personally, I consider a system *graphical* if it can recreate familiar objects through manipulation of individual pixels on the screen. Graphics, however, work only if the screen resolution makes these renditions realistic and natural. It's too bad graphics systems have an unspoken rule that always seems to spoil things: you either need more resolution than you have, or you need more colors. It goes hand in hand with the other famous memory postulate: you always need more memory than you have; otherwise, you need more speed.

Graphics makes everything more complicated than it would be in text mode. Even displaying a string on the screen requires several operations, such as initializing the graphics mode and selecting a font style, writing direction, text color, and background color. You also become responsible for erasing portions of the screen before writing something, unless you want to superimpose items. This extra work inevitably causes loss of speed. Fortunately, PCs are getting faster and graphics cards are becoming more powerful, so speed is rarely an overriding issue.

Considering the number of operations necessary, programmers need a class that hides these difficulties inside itself, providing a clean (and machine independent) interface. Class *Graphics* was written for this purpose. It uses the underlying Borland Graphics Interface (BGI) library functions of the Turbo C++ compiler to do the actual work. If you use the Zortech C++ compiler, its *flash graphics* library is used.

This book thus implements two separate versions for the *Graphics* class—one for Turbo C++ and one for Zortech C++. They have exactly the same interface, so the rest of the GUI is insensitive to the library used. This chapter describes the details of the Turbo C++ implementation, but the Zortech implementation is available on disk. To distinguish the two, this book saves the former in file "bgraphics.cpp" and the latter file "zgrahpics.cpp." They share a common header file, which chooses the source file to use based on a compiler switch.

The Screen Coordinate System

The BGI library functions implicitly use a left-handed Cartesian coordinate system. What this means is that the origin of the screen lies at the upper left corner. The Zortech library defines the origin as the lower left corner. Other systems may be different still. Application code must be allowed to use a consistent screen layout so that changing compilers or even machines will not be detrimental. In this book the screen follows the right-handed system, with the origin at the lower left. The Y axis increases toward the top of the screen, and the X axis increases toward the right. All coordinates given to and received from class *Graphics* will be converted to this format, just as for class *Mouse* in Chapter 1.

The *Graphics* class works with both EGA and VGA adaptors. The resolution of the screen was chosen to be 640 x 350, a common format for both cards. CGA adaptors are not supported.

The Graphics Library with Turbo C++

As stated, the *Graphics* class makes calls to the compiler graphics library. With Turbo C++ this means you have to link the code with the Turbo C++ file *graphics.lib*. Borland provides one graphics library for all memory models. At run-time the system needs a graphics device driver for the detected display adaptor. The code in class *Graphics* requires these drivers to be in the current directory. The project file "bdemo.prj" on the companion disk allow you to compile and link all the files needed automatically. All the files (except the Borland libraries) are available on the companion disk. To avoid copying the BGI device drivers into the current directory, you must modify the constructor for the *Graphics* class.

The Graphics Library with Zortech C++

The Zortech graphics libraries are contained in *fg?.lib*, where the *?* character is replaced by the character indicating the memory model of the compiler. The code in this book uses the medium memory model, so you need the *fgm.lib* file. Because Zortech doesn't use graphics device drivers, there is nothing more to add. Again, all the files necessary (except the Zortech libraries) are available on the included disk.

The Structure of Graphics Calls

When you call a member function of class *Graphics*, you need to supply *all* the attributes necessary to do the job. Although this seems fairly obvious, it's not. The BGI library functions use a different approach, in the interest of speed: you set attributes with certain functions, and the drawing functions use them implicitly thereafter. You don't have to pass the parameters around with each call. The problem is that you must always remember what the attributes are at any given time. If you set them every time you call a drawing function, you have defeated the purpose and your system will be slower than it should be. As a rule this book, which favors simplicity over speed, passes such required attributes as color and line style into every function that needs them. Besides, the difference in speed is slight for most situations. Many graphics functions that draw or fill large objects execute slowly. Adding one or two parameters to these function calls is usually not detrimental.

Graphics Functions Supported and Unsupported

The *Graphics* class handles only the most basic functions needed for the implementation of a GUI. It allows displaying circles, boxes, lines, and text; it shades items; and it makes 16 colors available. You can do a surprising amount of work with just these functions.

Although basic, they are very flexible. Many complex graphics objects are simply combinations of simpler ones made up by circles, rectangles, or lines. The ability to manipulate individual pixels on-screen enables you to fine-edit details of irregular objects. The graphics functions described in this chapter implemented all the demo program on the companion disk. By running the program you can see how much you can do with class *Graphics*.

Many of the graphics features used widely in GUIs I haven't implemented in class *Graphics*. I wanted to concentrate on some key issues of C++ implementation, without getting too carried away with details. Among the unsupported operations are the following:

Pattern-filling (*BitBlt* operations)

Color palette operations

Using variable text fonts

Many systems don't make use of these features, but inevitably some users need to add something to the class. In general this step isn't difficult. There are three ways to achieve it:

1. Add them to class *Graphics*.

2. Derive a new class from *Graphics* and add them there.

3. Write a completely new class.

The best way to add these is to extend class *Graphics*, because you have access to its source code. If the class were available only in compiled form (normally how vendors deliver C++ classes), you would derive a new class from *Graphics* and add your new features to it.

Now that you have studied some features of class *Graphics*, you are ready to see the details of its interface. The header file in listing 2.1 contains the declaration for the class.

Listing 2.1. The header file for class BGraphics.

```
#ifndef BGRAPHICHPP
#define BGRAPHICHPP

#include <graphics.h>
#include <iostream.h>
#include <stdlib.h>
#include <bios.h>


#define GRAY LIGHTGRAY
#define BRIGHT_RED LIGHTRED
#define BRIGHT_GREEN LIGHTGREEN
#define BRIGHT_BLUE LIGHTBLUE
#define BRIGHT_YELLOW YELLOW
#define BRIGHT_CYAN LIGHTCYAN
#define BRIGHT_MAGENTA LIGHTMAGENTA

typedef struct box_type {
   int x1, y1, x2, y2;
} BOX_TYPE;
```

```
typedef int COLOR_TYPE;

class Graphics {

    int screen_width, screen_height;
    int font_width, font_height;

public:

    Graphics();
    void DrawDot(int, int, int);
    void DrawBox(int, int, BOX_TYPE*);
    void DrawCircle(int, int, int, int, int);
    void DrawLine(int, int, BOX_TYPE*);
    void FillBox(int, BOX_TYPE*);
    void FillCircle(int, int, int, int);
    void PutString(int, int, int, char*);
    int FontWidth() {return font_width;}
    int FontHeight() {return font_height;}
    int ScreenWidth() {return screen_width;}
    int ScreenHeight() {return screen_height;}
    void Terminate();
    ~Graphics();
};

extern Graphics* GraphicsHandler;

#endif
```

The inclusion of file <*graphics.h*> will bring in all the Borland settings and #defines if the BORLAND macro is defined in file *constant.hpp*. This chapter declares several macros dealing with colors. This step is necessary because Turbo C++ or Zortech C++ defines these colors in slightly different manners and the rest of the GUI needed a coherent definition. The Zortech header file *zgraphics.hpp* has similar statements. Next is the declaration of the fundamental screen entity BOX_TYPE. This type denotes a rectangular area of the screen, but it doesn't have any three-dimensional connotations, except that it can be shaded. Nearly all screen objects are rectangular and use this structure. Boxes are also much quicker to draw than circles, ellipses, or irregular shapes, and they resemble commonly used objects much more. The coordinates (x1, y1) refer to a box's lower left corner, and the (x2, y2) refer to the upper right one, as shown below.

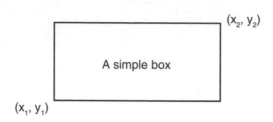

Fig. 2.1. The coordinates used to define a box.

Note that to define a rectangular area on-screen, you need only indicate the coordinates of two diagonally opposite corners of the area. This book uses the lower-left and the upper-right corner points. Of course, it takes more than two points to define an irregular (non-rectangular) screen area, but this book does not deal with objects of this type.to

Inside the class itself are four private variables, which record the screen and font characteristics detected at initialization time. The BGI library selects a default 8 x 8 pixel bit-mapped font. To find the length of a string in pixels, multiply the font width by the string length. You can't do this with the proportionally spaced fonts in the library. The variables *screen_width* and *screen_height* will be initialized to indicate a 640 x 350 layout. Listing 2.2 shows the code for class *BGraphics*.

Listing 2.2. The implementation of class BGraphics.

```
#include "bgraphic.hpp"

Graphics::Graphics()
{
    // detect the graphics card installed
    int gdriver = VGA;
    int gmode = VGAMED;

    initgraph(&gdriver, &gmode, "");
    if (graphresult() != grOk) {
      Terminate();
      cerr << "\nUnable to open graphics device";
      exit(1);
    }

    // compute the screen dimensions
    struct viewporttype screen;
    getviewsettings(&screen);
```

```
        screen_width = abs(screen. right - screen. left);
        screen_height = abs(screen. top - screen. bottom);

        // compute the size of a character
        font_width = textwidth("A");
        font_height = textheight("A");
}

void Graphics::DrawDot(int color, int x, int y)
{
        putpixel(x, screen_height - y, color);
}


void Graphics::DrawBox(int color, int style, BOX_TYPE* box)
{
        int polygon [10];
        polygon [0] = box->x1;
        polygon [1] = screen_height - box->y1;
        polygon [2] = box->x1;
        polygon [3] = screen_height - box->y2;
        polygon [4] = box->x2;
        polygon [5] = screen_height - box->y2;
        polygon [6] = box->x2;
        polygon [7] = screen_height - box->y1;
        polygon [8] = box->x1;
        polygon [9] = screen_height - box->y1;

        setlinestyle(style, 1, 1);
        setcolor(color);
        drawpoly(5, polygon);
}


void Graphics::DrawCircle(int color,
                int style,
                int x, int y, int radius)
{
        setcolor(color);
        setlinestyle(style, 1, 1);
        ellipse(x, screen_height - y, 0, 360, radius, radius);
}


void Graphics::DrawLine(int color, int style, BOX_TYPE* box)
{
        setcolor(color);
        setlinestyle(style, 1, 1);
        moveto(box->x1, screen_height - box->y1);
        lineto(box->x2, screen_height - box->y2);
}
```

Listing 2.2 Continues

37

Listing 2.2 Continued

```
void Graphics::FillBox(int color, BOX_TYPE* box)
{
    setcolor(color);
    setlinestyle(SOLID_LINE, 1, 1);
    setfillstyle(SOLID_FILL, color);

    int polygon [8];
    polygon [0] = box->x1;
    polygon [1] = screen_height - box->y1;
    polygon [2] = box->x1;
    polygon [3] = screen_height - box->y2;
    polygon [4] = box->x2;
    polygon [5] = screen_height - box->y2;
    polygon [6] = box->x2;
    polygon [7] = screen_height - box->y1;

    fillpoly(4, polygon);
}


void Graphics::FillCircle(int color, int x, int y, int
radius)
{
    setcolor(color);
    setlinestyle(SOLID_LINE, 1, 1);
    fillellipse(x, screen_height - y, radius, radius);
}


void Graphics::PutString(int color, int x, int y, char*
string)
{
    setcolor(color);
    settextjustify(LEFT_TEXT, BOTTOM_TEXT);
    outtextxy(x, screen_height - y, string);
}


void Graphics::Terminate()
{
    // exit graphics mode
    closegraph();
}

Graphics::~Graphics()
{
    // close the graphics mode
    Terminate();
}
```

Function Descriptions

Graphics::Graphics

The class constructor calls the BGI initialization function to establish a 640 x 350 screen in graphics mode. Class *Graphics* does not support CGA and monochrome adaptors. If this initialization is unsuccessful, the system aborts and returns to DOS after displaying an error message through C++ stream I/O on the standard error stream.

The screen attributes are read and stored for later use, as are the font characteristics. The screen shows nothing during this initialization.

Graphics::DrawDot

This is the simplest graphics function possible. All it does is display a single dot on the screen, using the requested coordinates and color. Note the conversion from left to right-handed system on the Y coordinate.

Graphics::DrawBox

This function and its cousin *FillBox* are the workhorses of most GUIs because of the predominance of rectangular objects on the screen. The BGI function *drawpoly* does the actual work. Note that to make a closed rectangle, you have to pass five points to describe it correctly. Passing just four points to *drawpoly* will result in a rectangle with the lower side missing. No filling is performed, and all the BGI line styles are available. Coordinates are converted into a right-handed system.

Graphics::DrawCircle

Although this book doesn't use circles in any GUI constructs, they may be necessary for the application program. The simplest way to define a circle is to indicate the coordinates of its center and the length of its radius. I also added the color attribute and the line style as usual. *DrawCircle* makes use of the more generic BGI ellipse function to do the actual drawing. Note the conversion from left to right-handed system on the Y coordinate.

Graphics::DrawLine

This function draws a straight line between the points (x1, y1) and (x2, y2), using a specific color and line style. Any of the BGI line styles is acceptable. To draw a horizontal line, the y coordinates must be the same. For a vertical line, the x coordinates must be equal.

Graphics::FillBox

As stated, this is one of the most used graphics functions. Although the BGI functions allow fill patterns other than solid colors, this book hasn't supported that feature here because it is not essential. The BGI function *fillpoly* does the job and receives only four points, in contrast with the five that *drawpoly* needed in *Graphics::DrawLine*. A class should hide users from these kinds of details. Note the conversion from a left to a right-handed system on the Y coordinate.

Graphics::FillCircle

If you draw a circle, you may want to fill it with color. I regard the drawing and filling operations as separate: ergo, the two functions *DrawCircle* and *FillCircle*. The BGI function *fillellipse* does both in one call. Note the conversion from a left to a right-handed system on the Y coordinate, as usual.

Graphics::PutString

This function displays a character string on the screen, using the graphics mode. Writing characters this way does *not* erase pixels that had been turned on previously in the same area. If you want a new string to replace an old one, the old one must be erased first by displaying it in the background color.

Graphics::FontWidth

This function returns the width of the letter "A" and is expressed in unit pixels. This function can be used to determine the width of a string, by multiplying the length of the string by the value returned by *Graphics::FontWidth()*. This technique is useful only with fonts for which all characters have the same width. Proportionally spaced fonts cannot be treated this way, but the fonts used in this book are all nonproportional. Borland C++ comes with a function called *textwidth(char*)* that can be used with proportional fonts. The function takes a pointer to a string and returns the overall width of the string in pixels.

Graphics::FontHeight

This function is the counterpart to the previous one.

Graphics::ScreenWidth

This function is used to determine the width of the screen in pixels. The initial screen width is set to 640 for EGA and VGA display adaptors, but application programs sometimes elect to change this at run-time, or they may be written to run with display adaptors with different screen resolutions.

Graphics::ScreenHeight

This function is the counterpart to the previous one. The screen height is initially set to 350 pixels.

Graphics::Terminate

This function terminates the graphics mode and reverts the screen to the mode it was in prior to creating the graphics handler. It uses the BGI function *closegraph()* to do the job, which releases any memory allocated for BGI use.

Graphics::~Graphics

The class destructor calls the previous function to deallocate the BGI memory and restore the screen.

3

The Screen Handler

The computer screen conveys all the GUI information to the user. Many objects fill the screen. They represent controls, readouts, text, etc. This book refers to them generically as icons. Somehow the GUI must coordinate the actions of all the icons displayed so that interaction with the user is both simple and intuitive. Clicking the mouse on an icon should activate that icon. Whenever the user types keys on the keyboard, the system should process them by routing them to a selected icon. A new class will be needed to handle all these tasks. This chapter will refer to it as *Screen* and describe it in detail later in this chapter.

You appreciate the full power and elegance of C++ inheritance here, because no subsequent objects derived from class *Icon* need knowledge of the inner screen-handling machinery.

In designing a system for flexibility, you should rely on techniques that yield the simplest and most elegant solutions. Because all objects displayed on the screen behave similarly, set up a class hierarchy of display objects that all derive from some fundamental or root class. This class ideally encapsulates all the complexities in handling keyboard or other events, leaving only simple, specialized tasks for the derived objects. As it turns out, the only significant function you can perform with the class *Icon* itself is registering the screen coordinates of the derived object. The screen manager must supply additional control structures capable of managing sets of icons.

The Root Class Icon

The *Icon* class is an abstract one because its only purpose is to act as a root base class for all displayable objects. Objects of *Icon* cannot display themselves and, in fact, have no physical consistency. To guarantee that objects of class Icon are never instantiated directly, the member function *Icon::Display()* is declared pure virtual, with the special assignment-operator notation. This declaration makes *Icon* an abstract C++ class, which in turn prevents *Icons* from direct use, except as a base class. The importance of *Icon* is that it provides a single, consistent, polymorphic interface for manipulation by class *Screen*. All operations on displayed objects are funnelled through it. It's ironic that the single most important part of the interface is also the simplest.

As stated, the functions provided directly by the class are limited because the interface, not the code itself, provides the power. The most interesting part of the class is what the header file contains.

Class *Screen* is declared a **friend** of *Icon* so that it can access the private coordinate variables needed for display-list processing. This solution seemed better than the alternative of providing a set of access-member functions in Icon. The display list is a doubly linked one with a reference to all icons displayed on-screen. It is described later in this chapter.

Next come the declarations of the screen-coordinate variables. Each icon requires only two coordinates to determine its size and location. This number is sufficient because all displayed objects are assumed to be delimited by a rectangular region. The x1 and y1 integers represent the lower left corner of the region. The x2 and y2 integers represent the upper right. Working with rectangular regions simplifies mouse and screen handling dramatically and is a common technique used by many commercial GUIs.

Note the empty virtual functions in the class. These functions provide a common entry point into derived objects. If you did *not* override particular functions, the base class *Icon* would intercept the function invocation and do nothing. See listings 3.1 and 3.2 for the header and source code files for class *Icon*.

Listing 3.1. The header file for class Icon.

```
#ifndef ICONHPP
#define ICONHPP

class Icon {

    friend class Screen;
```

```
protected:

    int x1, y1, x2, y2;
public:

    Icon(int, int, int, int);

    virtual void Display() = 0;
    virtual void Update() {}
    virtual void LeftButtonPressed() {}
    virtual void LeftButtonReleased() {}
    virtual void MiddleButtonPressed() {}
    virtual void MiddleButtonReleased() {}
    virtual void LeftButtonDragged(unsigned,
                            unsigned,
                            int) {}
    virtual void MiddleButtonDragged(unsigned,
                            unsigned,
                            int) {}
    virtual void KeyTyped(int) {}
    virtual ~Icon();
};

#endif
```

Listing 3.2. The implementation of class Icon.

```
#include "icon.hpp"
#include "screen.hpp"

Icon::Icon(int ix1, int iy1, int ix2, int iy2)
{
    x1 = ix1;
    y1 = iy1;
    x2 = ix2;
    y2 = iy2;

    CurrentScreen->AddItem(this);
}

Icon::~Icon()
{
    CurrentScreen->RemoveItem(this);
}
```

Function Descriptions

Icon::Icon

The class constructor saves the screen coordinates of the object. The object is then appended to the end of the display list. This constructor is invoked during the construction of derived objects, using the special base-class initializer syntax. Any object derived from class *Icon* is required to have a set of coordinates indicating the object's size and location. All objects are assumed to occupy a rectangular area on the screen. The point (x1, y1) designates the lower left corner; (x, y2) the upper right.

Icon::Display

This function is very special for class *Icon:* it is declared but not defined. Using the assignment operator in the function declaration in file icon.hpp, function *Icon::Display()* is declared a null virtual function. This declaration is necessary for two reasons. First, objects of class *Icon* are incapable of displaying themselves because the class itself contains no information regarding specific shape, color, or other details. Second, declaring class *Icon* to contain a null virtual function automatically makes the entire class abstract, which prevents the user from creating objects of class *Icon* directly. The class is designed to be used as a base class, and only derived objects know how to display themselves.

Icon::Update

This function provides objects with animation. It is called by the screen handler for each icon in the display list. Icons not capable of animation can simply ignore this function because its default behavior is to do nothing. If a class needs to be animated, it must be derived from *Icon* and override *Icon::Update()*. The interval between successive calls to the *Update* function for each icon is not guaranteed to be constant because it depends on the cycle time through the event loop in class *TopLevel*, shown in a later chapter. To provide animation at a rigorously constant rate, an object can use the function *Events::SystemTime()* to determine the amount of time elapsed between calls. This works well for icons that don't need to be updated too rapidly, because the resolution of *Events::SystemTime()* is one second. For higher resolution it is necessary to use the system tick timer, whose frequency is 18.2 Hz. For even faster animation, assuming that the hardware can update the GUI objects that fast, you need to either increase the frequency of the system tick (a task that is not without complications) or program the PC hardware timer chip explicitly.

Icon::LeftButtonPressed

This function processes clicking the left mouse button on an object. Not all objects need to respond to a mouse click; they can ignore this function.

Icon::LeftButtonReleased

As with the previous function, this one is invoked by the screen handler. Not all objects in a GUI are required to react to mouse commands, and for these objects you can simply ignore the functions *Icon::LeftButtonPressed()* and *Icon::LeftButtonReleased()*.

Icon:MiddleButtonPressed

This is the counterpart for the previous function LeftButtonPressed, but for the middle mouse button. Not all mice have a middle button — most have just a left and a right one.

Icon::MiddleButtonReleased

If you use a mouse with three buttons, this function will be called any time the middle button is released on an icon. With a two-button mouse, this function and the previous one are useless.

Icon::LeftButtonDragged

This function is designed to be used with icons that can be moved around on the screen by the user. Most objects are generally fixed in a GUI, but some can be resized or relocated, like the application windows in Microsoft Windows. Other GUIs support tear-off menus, relocatable tool icons, etc.

All of these use a function similar to *Icon::LeftButtonDragged()*. For objects that are designed *not* to be moved, this function should be ignored because its default behavior is to do nothing.

Icon::MiddleButtonDragged

This function is similar to the previous function *Icon::LeftButtonDragged()*.

Icon::KeyTyped

This is the only function that deals with the keyboard. Most traditional interfaces devote substantial amounts of processing to this part. The overall structure allows a simple solution: whenever you type a key, you send it to the icon with the input focus, as described in Chapter 1. This procedure is different from most systems', in which the application itself runs in a loop waiting for operator input through the interface (for example, Microsoft Windows).

Icon::~Icon

This virtual destructor removes the object from the screen list. During the sequence of events in the deletion of a derived object, the compiler automatically invokes this destructor after the derived class's destructor.

The DisplayList Class

When you design a system to handle large numbers of items in memory, there are two natural choices of data structures: arrays and lists. Because in a GUI the number of items to handle is not known in advance, the use of arrays is not a good choice unless they are dynamically allocated. Even so, the overhead required for inserting and removing items from the array and recompacting or expanding the array is excessive for even medium-size arrays. Moreover, arrays require blocks of contiguous storage, and for large arrays this may lead to a failure in the memory allocator at run-time.

Because of this, GUIs typically use linked lists to manage the objects on the screen. Linked lists are not as efficient as arrays because they require storage overhead for pointers and they are not randomly accessible. However, using lists is a straightforward process in C++ because the language handles the details of dynamic memory management with the operators *new* and *delete*. All objects to be displayed are inserted into a special doubly linked list. This list, usually referred to as the display list, is one-dimensional. It doesn't branch out in any direction, as shown in figure 3.1, and simply collects all the objects shown on the screen.

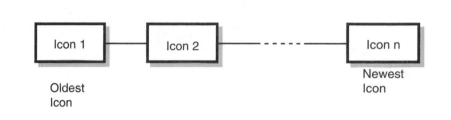

Fig. 3.1. The linear structure of the display list.

The simple linear structure makes processing easy. When an icon needs to be displayed, it is always inserted at the end of the list. This causes the list to contain items arranged in their chronological order of creation. Having a data structure in which a time relationship is implicitly encoded is important when dealing with user events, such as keypresses or mouse clicks.

The list order conveys on-screen to the user that icons at the end of the display list are "on top" of those at the beginning of the list. Imagine the icons as pieces of paper placed on a surface in the same order they have in the list. To determine if one object is "under" another one, you need to check only two things. An object of interest following another in the list certainly does not appear under the latter. And the screen coordinates of the icons indicate if earlier objects hide each other.

When processing mouse or keyboard events, the list structure turns out to be useful again. When the mouse is clicked on a pixel, the GUI needs to determine which icon that pixel belongs to. When multiple icons overlap each other on the screen at that particular point, the processing could easily become very messy. Traversing the linked list in the backward direction allows the system to find the most recent icon displayed that encloses the pixel in question.

This book's doubly linked list class does not use the Turbo C++ or the Zortech C++ supplied classes to guarantee portability. It declares the class *DisplayListNode* for the list-node objects. Each icon displayed attaches to its own node. Listing 3.3 shows the header file for class *DisplayList*, and listing 3.4 shows its implementation.

Listing 3.3. The header file for class DisplayList.

```
#ifndef LIST_MANAGER
#define LIST_MANAGER

#include <stdlib.h>
#include <stdio.h>

#include "icon.hpp"

class DisplayListNode {

    friend class DisplayList;
    DisplayListNode* predecessor;
    DisplayListNode* successor;
    Icon* entry;

public:

    DisplayListNode(Icon* item);
};

class DisplayList {

private:

    friend class DisplayListNode;
    DisplayListNode* first_item;
    DisplayListNode* current_item;
    long list_length;

    void DeleteCurrentNode();
    void FatalListError(char*);

public:

    DisplayList();
    long Size() {return list_length;}
    void AddItem(Icon* item);
    void RemoveItem(Icon* item);
    Icon* CurrentItem();
    void NextItem() {current_item =
                     current_item->successor;}
```

```
      void operator++() {NextItem();}
      void operatorñ() {current_item =
                       current_item->predecessor;}
      void GotoBeginning();
      void GotoEnd();
      ~DisplayList();
};

#endif
```

Listing 3.4. The implementation of class DisplayList.

```
#include "listmgr.hpp"

DisplayListNode::DisplayListNode(Icon* item)
{
      entry = item;
      predecessor = successor = 0;
}


DisplayList::DisplayList()
{
      // create a null list
      first_item = 0;
      current_item = 0;
      list_length = 0;
}

void DisplayList::AddItem(Icon* item)
{
      // create a new node
      DisplayListNode* node = new DisplayListNode(item);
      if (!node)
        // whoops ñ no memory left
        FatalListError("memory allocation failure");

      if (list_length == 0) {

        // make the node the list's first element
        first_item = node;

        // connect the root to itself, so the list
        // is circular
        first_item->predecessor =
            first_item->successor = first_item;
      }
```

Listing 3.4 Continues

Listing 3.4 Continued

```
    else if (list_length == 1) {
      // add a second node to the list
      first_item->predecessor = node;
      first_item->successor = node;
      node->successor = first_item;
      node->predecessor = first_item;
    }

    else {

      // splice the new node in right after
      // the current one
      node->predecessor = current_item;
      node->successor = current_item->successor;
      current_item->successor->predecessor = node;
      current_item->successor = node;
    }

    // update the list variables
    current_item = node;
    list_length++;
}

void DisplayList::RemoveItem(Icon* item)
{
    // search for the item in the list,
    // starting from the beginning
    GotoBeginning();
    for (int i = 0; i < list_length; i++, NextItem() )
    {

      // see whether the next icon in the display list
      // is the one you are looking for
      if (item == CurrentItem() ) {
        // it is: remove it from the display list
        DeleteCurrentNode();
        return;
      }
    }
}

void DisplayList::DeleteCurrentNode()
{
    // abort if no items in list
    if (current_item == 0)
      return;

    // remove the current item from the list
    current_item->predecessor->successor =
      current_item->successor;
    current_item->successor->predecessor =
      current_item->predecessor;
```

```
        // delete the item's parts
        current_item = current_item->successor;
        list_length--;
}

Icon* DisplayList::CurrentItem()
{
        // abort if no items in list
        if (current_item == 0)
            FatalListError("list access error");

        return current_item->entry;
}

void DisplayList::GotoBeginning()
{
        current_item = first_item;
}


void DisplayList::GotoEnd()
{
        current_item = first_item->predecessor;
}


void DisplayList::FatalListError(char* string)
{
        printf("\nDisplay List: ");
        printf("%s\n", string);
        exit(1);
}

DisplayList::~DisplayList()
{
        GotoBeginning();

        while (list_length)
          DeleteCurrentNode();
}
```

Function Descriptions

DisplayListNode::DisplayListNode

The class constructor for the list nodes attaches the referenced icon to the node and initializes the forward and backward link pointers to zero.

DisplayList::DisplayList

The list constructor creates no nodes but initializes the list variables. Attempting to reference an item in an empty list causes a run-time error.

DisplayList::AddItem

This function adds a node into the linked list. If no memory is available for dynamic allocation, an error message appears and the program terminates.

The item is added just after the one considered *current*, and then it becomes the *current* one. Adding a series of icons this way orders them chronologically in the list without repositioning the list pointers.

The forward and backward pointers of a single item put in the list reference themselves. Adding a second item requires breaking this self-referencing.

DisplayList::RemoveItem

This function searches through the display list for a specific icon. If it finds this icon, it removes the icon from the list; otherwise, it returns without issuing errors. If the same icon occurs more than once in the display list, (an error condition for the code in this book!), only the oldest one is removed, because the display list is traversed in a forward direction. A subsequent call to *DisplayList::RemoveItem(Icon*)* would get to the next oldest occurrence, and so on.

DisplayList::DeleteCurrentNode

The list item currently selected is removed and deleted. If no items exist in the list, the function exits without errors. After removing the item, the next entry becomes the *current* one, so that removing multiple items follows the chronological order of insertion in the list.

DisplayList::CurrentItem

This function returns a pointer to the currently selected item. Attempting to access empty lists results in a run-time error message.

DisplayList::NextItem

This function traverses the display list in the forward direction. It moves only from the current node to the next one. Because the list of icons is in chronological order, the effect is to reference the icon created next. If the list is empty, no errors occur. If you invoke the NextItem function when the list's current item is the last one, wrap-around occurs and the first icon in the list becomes the new current one.

DisplayList::operator++

This is a shorthand version for the previous function. Overloading the ++ operator treats the entire display list intuitively as a scalar data type.

DisplayList::operator--

This is similar to the previous function, except that the list is traversed backward.

DisplayList::GotoBeginning

This function rewinds the list to the first item created, if any. No errors occur if the list is empty.

DisplayList::GotoEnd

This function sets the list pointer to the last item created. If the list is empty, no errors are reported.

DisplayList::FatalListError

This function is the error handler used to report run-time errors detected during display list handling.

Here you find the traditional *printf()* function rather than stream I/O in *FatalListError* because of inconsistencies that exist between Turbo C++ and Zortech C++ in the stream I/O libraries. Detected errors display a message and compel the program to abort, because appropriate recovery actions are undetermined.

The Screen Class

As opposed to the *Icon* class, this class contains no virtual member functions. The class is not designed to be an interface class, but rather, to be used as a screen handler. Only one instance of class *Screen* is needed in a PC environment, although larger systems such as industrial process control may require multiple independent displays. In these cases a GUI would utilize more than one instantiation of class *Screen*.

The screen resolution supported by the GUI described in this book is fixed at compile time, by *#define* statements in the header file screen.hpp. This procedure limits flexibility but allows all the dimensions of the objects handled to be known *a priori*, thus considerably simplifying coordinate calculations. In a commercial GUI, the screen resolution is determined dynamically at run-time, and all the objects handled are displayed taking this resolution into account.

Most graphics libraries accomplish this step by calling special functions. Borland's BGI uses the functions *getmaxx()* and *getmaxy()* for this purpose. The Zortech flash graphics package contains the screen dimensions in a public structure called *fg*. This structure contains various global settings used inside the graphics package. The member *fg.displaybox* is a structure containing the size of the screen in pixels.

The most immediate limitation of using a fixed screen size is that both EGA and VGA systems have to use the same 640 x 350 screen layout. Many VGA cards allow resolutions up to 800 x 600 or even 1024 x 768, but these modes can't be supported unless run-time coordinates are used.

The screen uses a typical layout when displaying pages of icons. On the right is the page selector, which allows you to switch to a different page. On the top is an area often used to show the page title with perhaps the time and date or a company logo. Because most of these parts are repeated on every page, the invariant ones can be handled as a template directly by class *Screen*. The page title area changes with each page, so it's left to be handled by the *Page* class, described later on. Figure 3.2 shows a typical layout for a page.

The *Screen* class manages the icons on the display list, dispatching mouse or keyboard commands to them as needed. It controls writing and erasing of objects on the screen by dividing them into the three categories shown by the three areas in figure 3.2: work area, page selector, and title area. Each of these is described later. You can define as many areas as you want, such as a *dock* area like the one used in NeXTStep or an area for iconic painting tools. The class has separate member functions for dealing with each of the three categories. The header file for class *Screen* is shown in listing 3.5, and its implementation in listing 3.6.

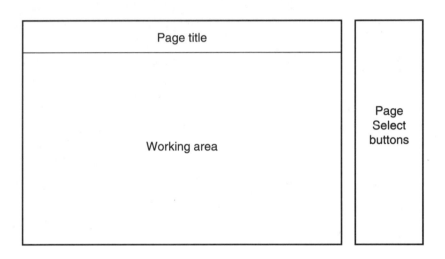

Fig. 3.2. The general layout of the screen.

Listing 3.5. The header file for class Screen.

```
#ifndef SCREENHPP
#define SCREENHPP

#include "icon.hpp"
#include "listmgr.hpp"
#include "legend.hpp"
#include "limit.hpp"
#include "pagesel.hpp"
#include "descrip.hpp"
#include "box.hpp"
```

Listing 3.5 Continues

Listing 3.5 Continued

```
#define SCREEN_X1 0
#define SCREEN_Y1 0
#define SCREEN_X2 639
#define SCREEN_Y2 349

#define WORK_PAGE_X1 1
#define WORK_PAGE_Y1 1
#define WORK_PAGE_X2 560
#define WORK_PAGE_Y2 349

#define SCREEN_TITLE_X1 0
#define SCREEN_TITLE_Y1 325
#define SCREEN_TITLE_X2 560
#define SCREEN_TITLE_Y2 349

#define PAGE_SELECTOR_X1 565
#define PAGE_SELECTOR_Y1 0
#define PAGE_SELECTOR_X2 639
#define PAGE_SELECTOR_Y2 439

class Screen {

        DisplayList display_list;      // list of all objects on
                                       // the screen
        Icon* work_area;               // points to page in work
                                       // area
        COLOR_TYPE background_color;   // of work page
        PageButtonArray* page;         // page selector buttons
        Icon* left_button_icon;        // last icon clicked

public:

        Screen();
        int NumberOfIcons() {return display_list. Size();}
        void DisplayTemplate();
        void ClearArea(int, int, int, int);
        void ClearWorkArea();
        void NewWorkArea(Icon*);
        void DisplayWorkArea();

        void ReDraw(int, int, int, int);
        void AddItem(Icon*);
        void RemoveItem(Icon*);
        void Update();
        void LeftButtonChanged(int, int, int);
        Icon* CurrentIcon(int x, int y);
        void LeftButtonDragged(int x, int y,
                        int delta_x, int delta_y,
                        int status);
        void KeyTyped(int, int, int);
```

```
     void SetPageButtonArray(PageButtonArray* pg)
          {page = pg;}
     PageButtonArray* GetPageButtonArray()
          {return page;}

     ~Screen();
};

extern Screen* CurrentScreen;

#endif
```

Listing 3.6. The implementation of class Screen.

```
#include "screen.hpp"

Screen::Screen()

{
     // define the global screen reference, so that the
     // individual screen subparts can be linked in before
     // the constructor returns
     CurrentScreen = this;

     // use a blue background for the work area
     background_color = BLUE;

     // create the page selector buttons
     page = new PageButtonArray();

     // start with no page selected
     work_area = 0;
}


void Screen::DisplayTemplate()
{
     // make the screen background gray
     BOX_TYPE screen;
     screen.x1 = SCREEN_X1;
     screen.y1 = SCREEN_Y1;
     screen.x2 = SCREEN_X2;
     screen.y2 = SCREEN_Y2;
     GraphicsHandler->FillBox(background_color, &screen);

     // display the page template
     page->Display();
}
```

Listing 3.6 Continues

Listing 3.6 Continued

```
void Screen::ClearArea(int x1, int y1, int x2, int y2)
{
     display_list. GotoBeginning();
     for (int i = 0;
           i < display_list.Size();
           i++, display_list++) {
       Icon* icon = display_list. CurrentItem();
       if (icon == 0) continue;

       // skip objects not in area of interest
       if (icon->x2 < x1) continue;
       if (icon->x1 > x2) continue;
       if (icon->y2 < y1) continue;
       if (icon->y1 > y2) continue;
       delete icon;
     }
}



void Screen::ClearWorkArea()
{
     if (work_area) {
       delete work_area;
       ReDraw(WORK_PAGE_X1, WORK_PAGE_Y1,
              WORK_PAGE_X2, WORK_PAGE_Y2);
       work_area = 0;
     }
}



void Screen::NewWorkArea(Icon* icon)
{
     work_area = icon;
}



void Screen::DisplayWorkArea()
{
     if (work_area)
       work_area->Display();
}



void Screen::ReDraw(int x1, int y1, int x2, int y2)
{
```

```
        // clear the selected screen area
        BOX_TYPE box;
        box.x1 = x1;
        box.y1 = y1;
        box.x2 = x2;
        box.y2 = y2;
        GraphicsHandler-> FillBox(background_color, &box);

        // go to the beginning of the display list
        display_list. GotoBeginning();

        // look for any icons invading the selected area
        for (int i = 0;
            i < display_list. Size();
            i++, display_list++) {

          // get the next icon from the display list
          Icon* icon = display_list. CurrentItem();
          if (icon == 0) continue;  // no icon: ignore it

          // skip objects not in area of interest
          if (icon->x2 < x1) continue;
          if (icon->x1 > x2) continue;
          if (icon->y2 < y1) continue;
          if (icon->y1 > y2) continue;

          // we found an icon that needs to be repainted.
          icon->Display();
        }
}

void Screen::Update()
{
        // go to the beginning of the display list
        display_list. GotoBeginning();

        // forward traverse the entire display list
        for (int i = 0;
            i < display_list. Size();
            i++, display_list++) {

          Icon* icon = display_list. CurrentItem();
          // ignore null icons
          if (icon == 0) continue;

          // attempt to update the icon
          icon->Update();
        }
}
```

Listing 3.6 Continues

Listing 3.6 Continued

```
void Screen::AddItem(Icon* icon)
{
     // go to the end of the display list
     display_list. GotoEnd();

     // insert the icon
     display_list. AddItem(icon);
}



void Screen::RemoveItem(Icon* icon)
{
     // search for menu window in screen_list
     // and delete it
     display_list. RemoveItem(icon);
}



void Screen::LeftButtonChanged(int x, int y, int status)
{
     if (status == MOUSE_LEFT_BUTTON) {
       // mouse button is pressed:
       // see what icon was hit
       left_button_icon = CurrentIcon(x, y);

       if (left_button_icon == 0) return;
       left_button_icon->LeftButtonPressed();
     }
     else {
       // mouse button was released
       if (left_button_icon == 0) return;
       left_button_icon->LeftButtonReleased();
     }
}

void Screen::LeftButtonDragged(int x, int y,
                        int deltax, int deltay, int status)
{
     // see if an icon was hit
     Icon* icon = CurrentIcon(x, y);
     if (icon == 0) return;

     // it was: invoke it
     icon->LeftButtonDragged(deltax, deltay, status);
}


Icon* Screen::CurrentIcon(int x, int y)
{
```

```
        Icon* object;

        // go to the end of the display list
        display_list. GotoEnd();

        // backward traverse the entire list
        for (int i = 0;
             i < display_list. Size();
             i++, display_listñ) {

          object = display_list. CurrentItem();

          // see if the mouse is inside this object
          if ( (x >= object->x1) && (x <= object->x2) ) {
            if ( (y >= object->y1) && (y <= object->y2) )

              // it is: return a pointer to the icon
              return object;
          }
        }
        /* no icon found: return a null pointer */
        return (Icon*) 0;
}



void Screen::KeyTyped(int x, int y, int key)
{
        Icon* icon = CurrentIcon(x, y);

        if (icon)
          icon->KeyTyped(key);
}



Screen::~Screen()
{
        delete page;
}
```

Function Descriptions

Screen::Screen

The class constructor creates a screen object and initializes all the fields in it.
Note that it doesn't display anything on the screen. Using the variable *this* is
necessary to establish the *CurrentScreen* reference before creating anything else
on the screen.

63

The variable *this* is specific to C++. It references the object being processed — you should use it sparingly, with great care.

Screen::NumberOfIcons

This simple in-line function returns the number of icons on the display list.

Screen::DisplayTemplate

This function clears the entire screen and draws the basic template for all pages. In this case, the only item shown is the page selector.

Screen::ClearArea

This function searches through the display list looking for icons that invade a certain area of the screen. They are removed from the list and deleted, but the screen is not repainted.

Screen::ClearWorkArea

This function clears the work area of the display by deleting all icons referenced in the work area. The work area is then blanked. Deleting the page object automatically deletes all the child icons on it as well. As you will see, the page object's destructor takes care of this problem.

Screen::NewWorkArea

This function assigns a new page to the work area. When a page is created, it needs to be attached to the screen handler. This is done by passing a pointer to the page object to function *Screen::NewWorkArea (Icon*)*.

Screen::DisplayWorkArea

This function displays the page assigned to the work area. Pages are not created inside class *Screen*, but they are kept track of. The *Screen* class has only one work area, so only one page can be displayed at a time. Displaying a page object results in the page template and all the page icons being painted.

Screen::ReDraw

This function restores the screen after closing a popup icon. It clears a selected section of the screen and selectively repaints only icons that invade that area.

Screen::Update

This is the driving function for object animation. This function needs to be called periodically inside the event loop so that animation can be run between events. This function calls *Icon::Update( )* for each object in the display list. Objects that don't support animation will do nothing via the default virtual function *Icon::Update( )*.

Screen::AddItem

This function adds an icon to the display list by inserting it at the end of the list.

Screen::RemoveItem

This function searches for a specific icon in the display list and removes it if found. If the item is not found in the list, no action is taken.

Screen::LeftButtonChanged

Pressing or releasing the left button on the mouse invokes this function. It searches through the display list for the icon that "owns" the pixel on which the mouse is located. To do this, it simply performs a backward traversing of the display list. When it finds an icon occupying the pixel in question, it invokes it.

Screen::LeftButtonDragged

This function moves on-screen objects around. The basic type of motion is that of cursor icons, but any derived icons can be endowed with the capability to be moved.

Screen::CurrentIcon

This function returns a pointer to the icon that occupies a specific pixel on the screen, if any. If many icons are overlapping on this pixel, the "one on top" is returned (that is, the last one created).

Screen::KeyTyped

This function routes any keys typed by the user to the icon with the input focus, determined by the coordinates of the last click of the left mouse button.

Screen::~Screen

This function deletes the page selector from the screen, the only object allocated dynamically inside the class *Screen*.

4

Simple Derived Classes

In a real GUI, lots of different types of objects need to be displayed and manipulated. Some respond to mouse or touch-screen commands, some are used only to display data, and some can be moved around. The overall structure of the GUI must accommodate these variations without being compromised and without lengthy rewriting of functions in derived objects. The full power of C++ is realized if a rational genealogy of simple classes is designed, in which each class adds only limited features to its parent class. Derived classes should have code only for methods that are added to the parent class, or actions that override functions in the parent.

Two basic types of icons in the GUI are described in this book: static and dynamic (not to be confused with statically and dynamically allocated objects!). Static icons maintain a fixed location on the screen, and are neither allowed to be moved or are capable of being moved. Dynamic icons, on the other hand, are designed for mobility. These two class types have the genealogy shown in Figure 4.1.

The simplest and most common control icons are static, which means mouse clicks can't move them around on the screen. They have no function for the event handler's invocation of *Icon::LeftButtonDragged*, which *Icon* intercepts itself. Even without mobility, static objects are useful and versatile. Status readouts, text messages, push buttons, and switches use them.

Most objects described in this book are static. Dynamic objects are different. You can click them and move them around within certain constrained areas. The cursors used in potentiometers are the most important dynamic objects this book covers. This chapter treats cursors; chapter 5 deals with potentiometers.

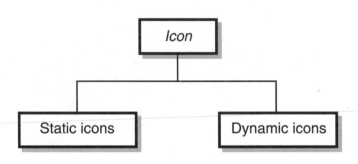

Fig. 4.1. The two object types.

This chapter describes the design and implementation of the following static icons:

- Boxes

- Legends

- Monostable push buttons

- Bistable push buttons

Figure 4.2 shows the genealogy for these objects

The Box and ShadedBox Classes

When you use graphics to draw controls on the screen, it makes sense to give the best graphical rendition possible. The controls implemented in this book make use of rectangular boxes to display themselves. Sometimes a simple box is used, other times a more complex one (shaded along the right and bottom edges, for example) is preferred. Although the additional effort to add shading is modest, the overall effect is quite pleasing. Shaded boxes are actually made up of two separate icons, as shown in Figure 4.3. You can draw even more realistic objects by using other techniques such as highlighting, pattern filling, and pixel editing, but these are nonessential for the purposes of this book.

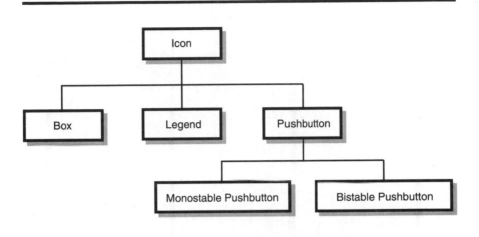

Fig. 4.2. The genealogy for some of the derived icons described in this chapter.

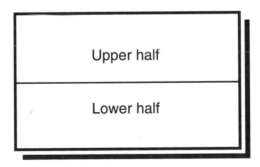

Fig. 4.3. The structure of a shaded box.

The reason for using separate icons to create a simple box is *reusability*. Other objects described throughout the book use these more primitive icons. As stated, each class should use as many features as possible from other classes. Listing 4.1 shows the header file for classes *Box* and *ShadedBox*.

Listing 4.1. The header file for Box *and* ShadedBox.

```
#ifndef BOXHPP
#define BOXHPP
#include "icon.hpp"
#include "graphics.hpp"

class Box: public Icon {

public:

        int x1, y1, x2, y2;
        COLOR_TYPE border_color;
        COLOR_TYPE fill_color;

        Box(int, int, int, int, COLOR_TYPE, COLOR_TYPE);
            virtual void Display();
              virtual void Color(COLOR_TYPE);
              virtual ~Box();
};



        class BottomShadedBox: public Icon {

          int x1, y1, x2, y2;
          COLOR_TYPE shade_color;
          COLOR_TYPE border_color;
          COLOR_TYPE fill_color;

public:

        BottomShadedBox(int, int, int, int,
              COLOR_TYPE, COLOR_TYPE, COLOR_TYPE);
        void Color(COLOR_TYPE);
        void Display();
};



        class TopShadedBox: public Icon {

          int x1, y1, x2, y2;
          COLOR_TYPE shade_color;
          COLOR_TYPE border_color;
          COLOR_TYPE fill_color;
```

```
public:

    TopShadedBox(int, int, int, int,
            COLOR_TYPE, COLOR_TYPE, COLOR_TYPE);
    void Color(COLOR_TYPE);
    void Display();
};


class ShadedBox: public Icon {

    BottomShadedBox* bottom_box;
    TopShadedBox* top_box;

public:

    ShadedBox(int, int, int, int,
            COLOR_TYPE, COLOR_TYPE, COLOR_TYPE);
    void Color(COLOR_TYPE);
    void Display();
    virtual ~ShadedBox();
};

#endif
```

The coordinates (x_1, y_1) define the lower left corner of a box. The coordinates (x_2, y_2) define the upper right corner. This convention is the same one used for all other icons described in this book. No destructors are in the classes *BottomShadedBox* and *TopShadedBox* because the destructor for the base class *Icon* is sufficient. The following pages show the actual C++ code for *ShadedBox* and related classes.

The local variables x1, y1, x2, y2 in the box classes may seem redundant because the base class Icon has exactly the same variables. The duplication is necessary, however, and here's why. Boxes displayed on the screen, whether shaded or not, have no behavior of their own and thus must never be activated by a mouse click or screen touch. Boxes are used only as support objects for the representation of more complex objects, such as pop-up windows or push-buttons. This implies that boxes should appear in the display list in a manner that doesn't interfere with mouse processing.

When an object uses a box to display itself, the box is created in the object's constructor, guaranteeing that the object itself will be inserted into the display list **before** the box. The problem is that in order to process a mouse click, the display list is traversed in the backward direction, and thus the box erroneously intercepts the command.

To overcome this problem I resorted to a small stratagem: box constructors pass the coordinates (-1, -1, -1, -1) to the base class *Icon*, thus appearing as a single off-screen point in the display list. Because boxes need to know their location and size, the screen coordinates had to be stored separately from class *Icon*. When the screen handler searches the display list, it skips over the box and invokes the correct object to handle the click: the object that created the box.

Listing 4.2. The complete implementation of Box *classes.*

```cpp
#include "box.hpp"

Box::Box(int rbx, int rby, int rbwidth, int rbheight,
                COLOR_TYPE border,
                COLOR_TYPE fill) :

        Icon(-1, -1, -1, -1)
{
        x1 = rbx;
        y1 = rby;
        x2 = x1 + rbwidth;
        y2 = y1 + rbheight;
        border_color = border;
        fill_color = fill;
}

void Box::Display()
{
        BOX_TYPE box;

        // fill inside of box
        box.x1 = x1;
        box.y1 = y1;
        box.x2 = x2 - 2;
        box.y2 = y2 - 2;
        GraphicsHandler->FillBox(fill_color, &box);

        // add border to box
        box.x1 = x1;
        box.y1 = y1;
        box.x2 = x2 - 1;
        box.y2 = y2 - 1;
        GraphicsHandler->DrawBox(border_color,
                                SOLID_LINE, &box);
}

void Box::Color(COLOR_TYPE color)
{
        fill_color = color;
}
```

```
ShadedBox::ShadedBox(int x,
         int y,
         int width,
         int height,
         COLOR_TYPE shade,
         COLOR_TYPE border,
         COLOR_TYPE fill) : Icon(-1, -1, -1, -1)
{
     bottom_box = new BottomShadedBox(x, y,
                        width, height / 2,
                        shade, border, fill);

     top_box = new TopShadedBox(x, y + height / 2,
                        width, height / 2,
                        shade, border, fill);
}

void ShadedBox::Display()
{
     bottom_box->Display();
     top_box->Display();
}

void ShadedBox::Color(COLOR_TYPE color)
{
     bottom_box->Color(color);
     top_box->Color(color);
}

ShadedBox::~ShadedBox()
{
     delete bottom_box;
     delete top_box;
}



BottomShadedBox::BottomShadedBox(int x,
         int y,
         int width,
         int height,
         COLOR_TYPE shade,
         COLOR_TYPE border,
         COLOR_TYPE fill) :    Icon(-1, -1, -1, -1)
{
     x1 = x;
     y1 = y;
     x2 = x1 + width;
     y2 = y1 + height;
```

Listing 4.2 Continues

Listing 4.2 Continued

```
        shade_color = shade;
        border_color = border;
        fill_color = fill;
}

void BottomShadedBox::Display()
{
    BOX_TYPE box;

    int x = x1;
    int y = y1;
    int width = x2 - x1;
    int height = y2 - y1;

    box.x1 = x + 2;
    box.y1 = y + 2;
    box.x2 = x + width - 3;
    box.y2 = y + height;

    // fill inside of box
    GraphicsHandler->FillBox(fill_color, &box);

    // add BOTTOM border lines
    BOX_TYPE bottom_border;
    bottom_border.x1 = x;
    bottom_border.y1 = y;
    bottom_border.x2 = x + width - 1;
    bottom_border.y2 = y + 1;
    GraphicsHandler->FillBox(border_color, &bottom_border);

    // add LEFT border lines
    BOX_TYPE left_border;
    left_border.x1 = x;
    left_border.y1 = y;
    left_border.x2 = x + 1;
    left_border.y2 = y + height - 1;
    GraphicsHandler->FillBox(border_color, &left_border);

    // add RIGHT border lines
    BOX_TYPE right_border;
    right_border.x1 = x + width - 2;
    right_border.y1 = y;
    right_border.x2 = x + width - 1;
    right_border.y2 = y + height - 1;
    GraphicsHandler->FillBox(border_color, &right_border);

    // add BOTTOM shade
    BOX_TYPE bottom_shade;
    bottom_shade.x1 = x + 2;
    bottom_shade.y1 = y - 4;
    bottom_shade.x2 = x + width + 3;
    bottom_shade.y2 = y  - 1;
    GraphicsHandler->FillBox(shade_color, &bottom_shade);
```

```
        // add RIGHT shade
        BOX_TYPE right_shade;
        right_shade.x1 = x + width;
        right_shade.y1 = y - 1;
        right_shade.x2 = x + width + 3;
        right_shade.y2 = y + height - 1;
      GraphicsHandler->FillBox(shade_color, &right_shade);
}

void BottomShadedBox::Color(COLOR_TYPE color)
{
        fill_color = color;
}




TopShadedBox::TopShadedBox(int x,
            int y,
            int width,
            int height,
            COLOR_TYPE shade,
            COLOR_TYPE border,
            COLOR_TYPE fill) :  Icon(-1, -1, -1, -1)
{
      x1 = x;
      y1 = y;
      x2 = x1 + width;
      y2 = y1 + height;

      shade_color = shade;
      border_color = border;
      fill_color = fill;
}

void TopShadedBox::Display()
{
        int x = x1;
        int y = y1;
        int width = x2 - x1;
        int height = y2 - y1;

        BOX_TYPE box;
        box.x1 = x + 2;
        box.y1 = y;
        box.x2 = x + width - 3;
        box.y2 = y + height - 3;

        // fill inside of box
        GraphicsHandler->FillBox(fill_color, &box);
```

Listing 4.2 Continues

Listing 4.2 Continued

```
    // add TOP border lines
    BOX_TYPE border;
    border.x1 = x;
    border.y1 = y + height - 2;
    border.x2 = x + width - 1;
    border.y2 = y + height - 1;
GraphicsHandler->FillBox(border_color, &border);

    // add LEFT border lines
    border.x1 = x;
    border.y1 = y;
    border.x2 = x + 1;
    border.y2 = y + height - 1;
GraphicsHandler->FillBox(border_color, &border);

    // add RIGHT border lines
    border.x1 = x + width - 2;
    border.y1 = y;
    border.x2 = x + width - 1;
    border.y2 = y + height - 1;
GraphicsHandler->FillBox(border_color, &border);

    // add RIGHT shade
    BOX_TYPE shade;
    shade.x1 = x + width;
    shade.y1 = y - 1;
    shade.x2 = x + width + 3;
    shade.y2 = y + height - 6;
GraphicsHandler->FillBox(shade_color, &shade);
}

void TopShadedBox::Color(COLOR_TYPE color)
{
    fill_color = color;
}
```

Function Descriptions

Box:Box

The class constructor passes the coordinates of the off-screen point (-1, -1) to the base class *Icon*. This action ensures that the class constructor does not show up on the display list during mouse processing. A set of variables private to class *Box* stores the actual box coordinates. In addition, there are two variables for the box colors: one for the color of the enclosing rectangle and one for the inside area. The constructor does *not* paint anything on the screen.

Box::Display

This function uses the graphics handler to display a rectangle filled with the appropriate color.

Box::Color

This function changes the color subsequently available in *Box::Display*. It does not paint anything on the screen.

BottomShadedBox::BottomShadedBox

This constructor is analogous to the one for class *Box*.

BottomShadedBox::Display

This function handles all the graphical details for painting the box on the screen. It uses the *Graphics* object's *FillBox* function to display itself. The box is shaded on the right and bottom edges.

BottomShadedBox::Color

This function changes the fill-color attribute of the box, but it does *not* modify or repaint the screen with the new color. This job is left to the function *BottomShadedBox::Display*.

TopShadedBox::TopShadedBox

TopShadedBox::Display

TopShadedBox::Color

These functions are similar to those described in class *BottomShadedBox*.

ShadedBox::ShadedBox

This constructor receives the coordinates of the lower left corner of the box, along with the width and the height. Shaded boxes have an inside *fill* color, a border color, and a shade color. The shading applies only to the right and the bottom sides of the box. All the parameters pass on to the two child classes created. No objects show up on the screen.

ShadedBox::Display

This, too, is a simple function. It passes along the *Display* command to its child objects. The function's only side effect is to display the shaded box on the screen at the position set at creation time.

ShadedBox::Color

This function changes the fill-color attribute of the box, but it does *not* modify or repaint the screen with the new color.

ShadedBox::~ShadedBox

The class destructor reclaims the memory allocated to the child objects and removes the icons from the display list. The display is *not* updated.

The Legend Class

The *Legend* class supports the display of text characters in graphics mode. Text commonly needs to be displayed inside a designated area of the screen to show the setting of a page, the name of a control, and so on. Given an area to display text in, three alignment commands are sufficient to handle most cases. The most commonly used one is *Center*. All the titles shown on pages, buttons, push buttons, and selectors show up with the *Legend::Center* function. The class itself is simple. Listing 4.3 shows its header file.

Listing 4.3. The header file for class Legend.

```
#ifndef LEGENDHPP
#define LEGENDHPP

#include <string.h>
#include <math.h>

#include "icon.hpp"
#include "graphics.hpp"

class Legend {

public:

    void Center(BOX_TYPE*, COLOR_TYPE, char*, char* = 0);
    void Left(BOX_TYPE*, COLOR_TYPE, char*, char* = 0);
    void Right(BOX_TYPE*, COLOR_TYPE, char*, char* = 0);0
};

#endif
```

All the member functions display their string arguments in a rectangular screen area. Multiple strings are equally spaced vertically in the box. Class *Legend* is different from most other classes in this book because it doesn't derive from class *Icon*; hence, it has no connections with the display list. This means it cannot respond to mouse clicks, and the screen manager never detects it.

Class *Legend* provides a purely aesthetic function (displaying characters) with no other behavior or purpose. Thus, the class has no variables, no base classes, and therefore no constructor or destructor functions, as shown in listing 4.4.

Listing 4.4. The implementation of class Legend.

```
#include "legend.hpp"

void Legend::Center(BOX_TYPE* box, COLOR_TYPE color,
                char* legend1, char* legend2)
{
    // compute width and height of area where text will go
    int width  = box->x2 - box->x1;
    int height = box->y2 - box->y1;

    // look up the size of each character
    int c_width  = GraphicsHandler->FontWidth();
    int c_height = GraphicsHandler->FontHeight();
```

Listing 4.4 Continues

Listing 4.4 Continued

```
        char* string [3];
        string [0] = legend1;
        string [1] = legend2;

        // determine actual number of arguments
        int legends;
        if (legend2)
          legends = 2;
        else
          legends = 1;

        for (int i = 0; i < legends; i++) {
          int x = box->x1 + \
                  (width - c_width * strlen(string [i]) ) / 2;
          int y = box->y1 + \
                  (legends - i) * \
                  height / (legends + 1) - c_height / 2;
          GraphicsHandler->PutString(color, x, y, string [i]);
        }
    }

    void Legend::Left(BOX_TYPE* box, COLOR_TYPE color,
                  char* legend1, char* legend2)
    {
      // compute width and height of area where text will go
      int height = box->y2 - box->y1;

      // look up the size of each character
      int c_height = GraphicsHandler->FontHeight();

      char *string [3];
      string [0] = legend1;
      string [1] = legend2;

      // determine actual number of arguments
      int legends;
      if (legend2)
        legends = 2;
      else
        legends = 1;

      for (int i = 0; i < legends; i++) {
        int x = box->x1;
        int y = box->y1 + \
              (legends - i) * \
              height / (legends + 1) - c_height / 2;
        GraphicsHandler->PutString(color, x, y, string [i]);
      }
```

```
}

void Legend::Right(BOX_TYPE* box, COLOR_TYPE color,
            char* legend1, char* legend2)
{
     // compute width and height of area where text will go
     int width  = box->x2 - box->x1;
     int height = box->y2 - box->y1;

     // look up the size of each character
     int c_width  = GraphicsHandler->FontWidth() + 1;
     int c_height = GraphicsHandler->FontHeight();

     char *string [3];
     string [0] = legend1;
     string [1] = legend2;

     // determine actual number of arguments
     int legends;
     if (legend2)
       legends = 2;
     else
       legends = 1;

     for (int i = 0; i < legends; i++) {
       int x = box->x1 + \
               width - c_width * strlen(string [i]);
       int y = box->y1 + \
               (legends - i) * \
               height / (legends + 1) - c_height / 2;
       GraphicsHandler->PutString(color, x, y,
string [i]);
     }
}
```

Function Descriptions

Legend::Center

This function displays one or two strings, center-aligned inside a rectangular screen area. Two strings show up one above the other, equally spaced between the top and bottom limits.

Legend::Left

This function displays one or two strings, left-aligned inside a rectangular screen area. Two strings show up one above the other, equally spaced between the top and bottom limits.

Legend::Right

This function displays one or two strings, right-aligned inside a rectangular screen area. Two strings show up one above the other, equally spaced between the top and bottom limits.

The PushButton Class and Its Siblings

A push button is the simplest control for setting and resetting a boolean variable. Push buttons can be either monostable or bistable. The former kind remains ON only while clicked, deactivating when released. The latter kind toggles from ON to OFF or vice versa when clicked. Otherwise, the controls look the same on-screen. Some applications require them to look different, easily accomplished by overloading the *Display* function instead of relying on *PushButton::Display* to do the work. Listings 4.5 and 4.6 show the header file and the code for the class. The variable "legend" is where the button's description string is saved. The integer pointer "state" references the boolean variable toggled by the button. It is the sole application variable manipulated by the icon. Pressing the button invokes an application program function (if defined) through the function pointer *activation_function*. Class *PushButton* is the first one in this book with such a function.

Listing 4.5. The header file for class PushButton.

```
#ifndef PUSHBUTTONHPP
#define PUSHBUTTONHPP

#include <string.h>

#include "icon.hpp"
#include "box.hpp"
#include "limit.hpp"
```

```cpp
#include "graphics.hpp"
#include "legend.hpp"

#define PUSH_BUTTON_WIDTH 70
#define PUSH_BUTTON_HEIGHT 30

class PushButton: public Icon {

protected:

    char legend [MAX_LEGEND_LENGTH + 1];
    int *state;
    void (*activation_function)();
    ShadedBox* box;

    COLOR_TYPE shade_color;
    COLOR_TYPE border_color;
    COLOR_TYPE fill_color;
    COLOR_TYPE inactive_color;
    COLOR_TYPE active_color;
    COLOR_TYPE legend_color;

public:

    PushButton(int, int, char*, int*, void(*)() );
    int CurrentState() {return *state;}
    void SetLegend(char* string)
      {strncpy(legend, string, sizeof(legend) );}
    virtual void Update() {}
    virtual void LeftButtonPressed() {}
    virtual void LeftButtonReleased() {}
    virtual void Display();
    void Activate();
    virtual ~PushButton();
};

class BistablePushButton: public PushButton {

public:

    BistablePushButton(int, int, char*, int*, void (*)() );
    virtual void Update() {}
    void LeftButtonPressed();
};

class MonostablePushButton: public PushButton {

public:

    MonostablePushButton(int, int, char*, int*, void (*)() );
```

Listing 4.5 Continues

Listing 4.5 Continued

```
        virtual void Update() {}
        void LeftButtonPressed();
        void LeftButtonReleased();
};

#endif
```

Listing 4.6. The implementation of class PushButton.

```
#include "pushbut.hpp"

PushButton::PushButton(int x, int y,
                        char* plegend,
                        int* initial_state,
                        void (*activate)() ) :
    Icon(x, y,
         x + PUSH_BUTTON_WIDTH,
         y + PUSH_BUTTON_HEIGHT)
{

    // save reference to the buttons's control variable
    state = initial_state;

    // also save the reference the application
    // program's function that will be invoked
    // when the button is used
    activation_function = activate;

    // record all the button colors
    shade_color = BLACK;
    border_color = BRIGHT_GREEN;
    inactive_color = CYAN;
    active_color = BRIGHT_CYAN;
    legend_color = BLUE;

    // set the initial color for the button
    fill_color = active_color;

    //record the botton's legend
    SetLegend(plegend);

    // create the backdrop box
    box = new ShadedBox(x1, y1,
                  x2 - x1, y2 - y1,
                  shade_color,
                  border_color,
                  fill_color);
}

void PushButton::Display()
{
```

```
        if (*state)
           fill_color = active_color;
         else
           fill_color - inactive_color;

        // show the backdop box
        box->Color(fill_color);
        box->Display();

        // display the push button legend
        BOX_TYPE box;
        box.x1 = x1;
        box.y1 = y1;
        box.x2 = x2;
        box.y2 = y2;
        Legend title_legend;
        title_legend.Center(&box, legend_color, legend);
}

void PushButton::Activate()
{
        // see if the button has an application
        // function to call, and invoke it if so
        if (activation_function)
          (*activation_function)();
}

PushButton::~PushButton()
{
        delete box;
}




BistablePushButton::BistablePushButton(int x, int y,
     char *legend, int* initial_state, void (*activate)() ) :
          PushButton(x, y, legend, initial_state, activate)
{}


void BistablePushButton::LeftButtonPressed()
{
        // toggle the button's state

        if (*state == 0) {
          // switch button to ON state
          *state = 1;
          fill_color = active_color;
        }
```

Listing 4.6 Continues

Listing 4.6 Continued

```
      else {
        // switch button to OFF state
        *state = 0;
        fill_color = inactive_color;
      }

      // change the button's color
      box->Color(fill_color);
      Display();

      // invoke the application program
      // to handle the button command
      Activate();
}
```

```
MonostablePushButton::MonostablePushButton(int x, int y,
  char *legend, int* initial_state,  void (*activate)() ) :
    PushButton(x, y, legend, initial_state, activate)
{}


void MonostablePushButton::LeftButtonPressed()
{
    // turn button ON
    *state = 1;
    fill_color = active_color;

    // show new button color
    box->Color(fill_color);
    Display();

    // invoke the application program
    // to handle the button command
    Activate();
}

void MonostablePushButton::LeftButtonReleased()
{
    // turn button OFF
    *state = 0;
    fill_color = inactive_color;

    // show new button color
    box->Color(fill_color);
    Display();

    // invoke the application program
    // to handle the button command
    Activate();
}
```

Function Descriptions

PushButton::PushButton

This function implements the generic button class. It is used as a base class for both *BistablePushButton* and *MonostablePushButton*. It registers the passed parameters and creates a shaded box for use as a backdrop. This constructor does *not* display anything on-screen.

PushButton::Display

This function is used to display objects of class *MonostablePushButon* and *BistablePushButton*. A shaded box displayed with a legend indicates the name of the button.

PushButton::Activate

The derived classes *BistablePushButton* and *MonostablePushButton* invoke this function. Theses classes use *PushButton::Activate* to call an application-specific function when you click them. If the button has no activation function attached, nothing happens. Application programs that constantly monitor all their interface variables sometimes do without activation functions for their controls.

PushButton::~PushButton

The backdrop box is deleted, but the screen is *not* updated to reflect this. The process of erasing objects from the screen, thus restoring it to some previous state, is the responsability of the screen handler or of a popup object. The former was treated in chapter 3, the latter in chapter 9.

BistablePushButton::BistablePushButton

A bistable control has two states, both stable; clicking the object causes a change in state. To change the state back, click it again. From active it becomes inactive or vice versa.

The constructor for a bistable button can use all the features of class *PushButton*; thus, the only action taken here is passing the state variables to the base class.

BistablePushButton::LeftButtonPressed

This function causes the button to change color, going from the ON to the OFF state or vice versa. The application program handler is also invoked. When you click a bistable icon, the sequence of function calls from the EventsHandler is:

1. Screen::LeftButtonChanged

2. BistablePushButton::LeftButtonPressed

3. PushButton::Display

4. PushButton::Activate

Notice how the class invokes the two functions *Display* and *Activate* of the base class and without using the scope-resolution operator. This action is possible because *BistablePushButton* has no declaration for functions of the same name.

MonostablePushButton::MonostablePushButton

A monostable control is similar to a bistable one, except that only one state is stable (usually the inactive one). Clicking it causes it to switch to the active state, but it goes back to the inactive one as soon as it is released.

Because class *PushButton* contains all necessary processing to create a monostable control, the constructor's sole function is to pass some arguments to the base class.

MonostablePushButton::LeftButtonPressed

This function is slightly different from the one in *BistablePushButton*. Here the button state is unconditionally set to ON. This type of button is ON when touched or clicked, and OFF when released. When you click a monostable icon, the sequence of function calls from the EventsHandler is the same as that for class *BistablePushButton*, as shown here:

1. Screen::LeftButtonChanged

2. MonostablePushButton::LeftButtonPressed

3. PushButton::Display

4. PushButton::Activate.

Notice how this class also invokes the two functions *Display* and *Activate* of the base class.

MonostablePushButton::LeftButtonReleased

This function unconditionally switches the button back to its OFF state. Unclicking (releasing the left mouse button) a monostable icon, the sequence of function calls from the EventsHandler is:

1. Screen::LeftButtonChanged

2. MonostablePushButton::LeftButtonReleased

3. PushButton::Display

4. PushButton::Activate.

The Cursor Class

The most important icon capable of moving around on the screen is the *Cursor*. In general a cursor is a mobile object used as a reference mark, like the cursor on your computer screen. Potentiometers need cursors to set levels. In this implementation, potentiometers need cursors capable of vertical or horizontal motion. For overall flexibility, cursors should theoretically be able to move anywhere on-screen.

Class *Cursor* is different from those previously shown because it is *child* class. This means it is used exclusively inside other classes to realize sub-parts of them. In this case class *Cursor* is a child of class *Potentiometer*, described later.

Potentiometers (described later) are controls used to adjust variables. For now, suffice it to say that potentiometers are complex icons which utilize several child objects. A child object is one used exclusively within the context of a greater object, referred to as the parent object. Child objects normally have very limited capabilities and let the parent do most of the processing. For example, when a *Cursor* object is moved, it doesn't know why it was moved or even what kind of parent icon it belongs to. A *Cursor* object knows only the limits of travel that the parent has set for it, and— using this limited knowledge—communicates to the parent class a new setting value for the potentiometer.

The class declaration shown in listing 4.7 can be found in the file pot.hpp. The first variable is a reference to the parent icon, to be notified when the cursor is used. Next come both the limits of travel in the x and y direction and the dimensions of the cursor. These were added so that cursors of any size can be created. The size is not critical, but horizontal and vertical cursors are oriented differently and move in different directions. A horizontal cursor moves in the horizontal direction, and is taller than it is wide. Both horizontal and vertical cursors can be seen in the demo program. Notice the declaration of the three private member functions *Blank*, *DisplayOutline*, and *UnDisplayOutline*. These functions are used when the cursor is dragged and are not accessible from outside the class.

Listing 4.7. The declaration of class Cursor.

```
class Cursor: public Icon {

    Pot* parent;

    int minimum_x, minimum_y;
    int maximum_x, maximum_y;
    int width, height;

    COLOR_TYPE shade_color;
    COLOR_TYPE border_color;
    COLOR_TYPE fill_color;
    COLOR_TYPE background_color;

    void Blank();
    void DisplayOutline();
    void UnDisplayOutline();

public:

    Cursor(Pot*, int, int, int, int, int, int,
           COLOR_TYPE);
    void Display();
    void LeftButtonPressed();
    void LeftButtonReleased();
    void LeftButtonDragged(unsigned delta_x,
                           unsigned delta_y,
                           int status);
};
```

A newly created cursor doesn't know whether the parent potentiometer allows it to move horizontally or vertically. The parent specifies its size and the dimensions of the rectangular area it can move in, and this determines its motion. The constructor for *Cursor* passes off-screen co-ordinates to *Icon* because the actual position of the cursor is unknown until part of the constructor code is executed.

The parent's *setting* is a pointer to a floating-point number that may vary between 0 and 1. It tells the cursor where to display itself inside its area. A 0 means it's at the bottom or left of it, and a 1 means it's at the top or right of it. The value of *setting* and the cursor position have a direct relation. The *Cursor* constructor uses *setting* to determine its position at creation time. When you move the cursor, its new position determines the new value of *setting*.

Cursors are displayed as shaded boxes, highlighted along the left and top sides. To make cursor objects capable of rapid motion on the screen, they must be easy to erase and repaint. For this purpose, only a dotted silhouette of the box is displayed while the cursor is clicked on. When the mouse button is released, the cursor is repainted in its more elaborate form. Listing 4.8 shows the implementation of class *Cursor*, which can be found in file pot.cpp.

Listing 4.8. The implementation of class Cursor.

```
Cursor::Cursor(Pot* parent_pot,
               int cwidth, int cheight,
               int min_x, int min_y, int max_x, int max_y,
               COLOR_TYPE background_clr) :

    Icon(-1, -1, -1, -1)
{
    // save a reference to our parent potentiometer
    parent = parent_pot;

    // maintain a copy of the cursor dimensions
    width = cwidth;
    height = cheight;

    // ... and the limits of motion
    minimum_x = min_x;
    minimum_y = min_y;
    maximum_x = max_x;
    maximum_y = max_y;

    // get the initial setting of the potentiometer
    float value = parent->Setting();
```

Listing 4.8 Continues

Listing 4.8 Continued

```
    // see whether cursor moves horizontally or vertically
    // and compute the initial screen location of the
    // cursor
    if (height > width) {
      // it moves horizontally
        x1 = minimum_x + value * (maximum_x - minimum_x);
        y1 = minimum_y;
    }
    else {
      // it moves vertically
      x1 = minimum_x;
      y1 = minimum_y + value * (maximum_y - minimum_y);
    }

    // update the cursor coordinates
    x2 = x1 + width;
    y2 = y1 + height;

    // record the color attributes
    shade_color = BLACK;
    border_color = RED;
    fill_color = GRAY;
    background_color = background_clr;
}

void Cursor::Display()
{
    // fill inside of cursor
    BOX_TYPE box;
    box.x1 = x1;
    box.y1 = y1 + 1;
    box.x2 = x2 - 1;
    box.y2 = y2 - 1;
    GraphicsHandler->FillBox(fill_color, &box);

    // highlight top of cursor
    box.x1 = x1;
    box.y1 = y2;
    box.x2 = x2 - 1;
    box.y2 = y2;
    GraphicsHandler->FillBox(WHITE, &box);

    // highlight left side of cursor
    box.x1 = x1;
    box.y1 = y1 + 2;
    box.x2 = x1;
    box.y2 = y2;
    GraphicsHandler->FillBox(WHITE, &box);
```

```
        // shade right side of cursor
        box.x1 = x2;
        box.y1 = y1;
        box.x2 = x2;
        box.y2 = y2 - 1;
        GraphicsHandler->FillBox(shade_color, &box);

        // shade bottom of cursor
        box.x1 = x1 + 1;
        box.y1 = y1;
        box.x2 = x2;
        box.y2 = y1 + 1;
        GraphicsHandler->FillBox(shade_color, &box);
}

void Cursor::Blank()
{
        BOX_TYPE box;

        // blank out the cursor, making it invisible
        box.x1 = x1;
        box.y1 = y1;
        box.x2 = x2;
        box.y2 = y2;
        GraphicsHandler->FillBox(background_color, &box);
}

void Cursor::DisplayOutline()
{
        BOX_TYPE box;

        // repaint the cursor, showing it as a
        // dotted outline
        box.x1 = x1;
        box.y1 = y1;
        box.x2 = x2;
        box.y2 = y2;
        GraphicsHandler->DrawBox(WHITE, DOTTED_LINE, &box);
}

void Cursor::UnDisplayOutline()
{
        BOX_TYPE box;

        // erase the dotted outline
        box.x1 = x1;
        box.y1 = y1;
        box.x2 = x2;
        box.y2 = y2;
        GraphicsHandler->DrawBox(background_color,
                                 DOTTED_LINE, &box);
}
```

Listing 4.8 Continues

Listing 4.8 Continued

```
void Cursor::LeftButtonPressed()
{
    // repaint the entire parent, in case
    // it was partially obscured by an icon.
    parent->Display();

    // erase the cursor
    Blank();

    // and replace it with the dotted outline
    DisplayOutline();
    EventsHandler->ShowMouseCursor();
}

void Cursor::LeftButtonReleased()
{
    UnDisplayOutline();
    EventsHandler->HideMouseCursor();
    Display();
    EventsHandler->ShowMouseCursor();
}

void Cursor::LeftButtonDragged(unsigned x, unsigned y,
                               int status)
{
    int new_x, new_y;

    // see if it moved in the X direction
    if (x) {
      new_x = x1 + x;
      if ( (new_x >= minimum_x) && (new_x <= maximum_x) ) {
        EventsHandler->HideMouseCursor();
        UnDisplayOutline();
        x1 = new_x;
        x2 = x1 + width;
        DisplayOutline();
        parent->Setting( \
         (float) (new_x - minimum_x) / \
              (maximum_x - minimum_x) );
        parent->SettingDisplay();
        EventsHandler->ShowMouseCursor();
      }
    }

    // see if it moved in the Y direction
    if (y) {
      new_y = y1 + y;
      if ( (new_y >= minimum_y) && (new_y <= maximum_y) ) {
        EventsHandler->HideMouseCursor();
        UnDisplayOutline();
```

```
y1 = new_y;
y2 = y1 + height;
DisplayOutline();
parent->Setting( \
 (float) (new_y - minimum_y) / \
         (maximum_y - minimum_y) );
parent->SettingDisplay();
EventsHandler->ShowMouseCursor();
      }
    }
  }
```

Function Descriptions

Cursor::Cursor

The class constructor registers all the state variables and determines whether the object can move vertically or horizontally. Notice that the coordinates passed to the base class are those of an off-screen point. The reason is that the cursor can determine its correct location on-screen only when it knows the value of the potentiometer setting.

Cursor::Display

This displays the cursor as a rectangular box, highlighted on the left and top edges. The right and bottom sides are shaded.

Cursor::Blank

This private function erases the cursor from the screen, but otherwise leaves the object undisturbed in memory.

Cursor::DisplayOutline

This private function draws a dotted box in place of the complete cursor icon so it can be moved around with less computation overhead.

Cursor::UnDisplayOutline

This private function erases the dotted cursor outline. Its advantage over *Blank* is its speed with large cursor objects. Because the inside of a cursor is already set to the background color, it is useless to fill the entire area.

Cursor::LeftButtonPressed

The display-list manager calls this function when the user touches a cursor or clicks the left mouse button on one. It changes the cursor into a dotted box.

Cursor::LeftButtonReleased

This function makes that cursor revert to its original appearance.

Cursor::LeftButtonDragged

This function actually makes a cursor move around. It tracks mouse movements by erasing the dotted box outline and redisplaying it at a new location, and it supports both vertical and horizontal motion. Notice how the function does *not* loop on itself to track the mouse, as some systems do. The top-level function remains in charge, a requirement for animation to work correctly. The function is called only when the event handler detects a mouse movement.

5

Compound Derived Classes

The controls in Chapter 4 are easy to build, use, and modify, but they have limitations. To build more powerful objects, there are really two alternatives: make more complicated objects or combine several simple objects together. This last approach leads to the subject of this chapter: compound objects.

Consider a commonly used control used in GUIs to adjust variables: the slider potentiometer, shown in figure 5.1. It is made up by several sub-objects called child objects, all coordinated by a single parent object. Moving the potentiometer's cursor results in a series of messages being passed around the object, as shown in figure 5.2. Because of the intimate relationship between the parent and children, the child classes are often declared **friend** to the parent. Using the compound-object approach yields simple child objects that are not only easy to debug but also usable with different kinds of parent without modification, if properly designed. The following sections describe several compound objects.

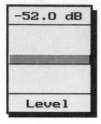

Fig. 5.1. An example of a compound object: a potentiometer.

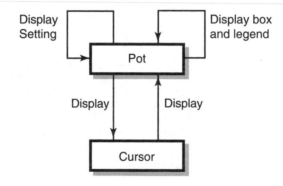

Fig. 5.2. The message sequence when mouse's left button is clicked on a pot cursor.

The Potentiometer Class

Most people don't know the term *potentiometer* but know how to use one. The volume control on your radio is probably a potentiometer, which this book refers to simply as a pot from now on. Any control with a smoothly rotating knob is probably a pot. Pots continuously adjust the level of analog variables. Pots have many applications, and practically any analog signal can be associated with one. A pot's behavior can be, for example, linear (such as a television's brightness control) or logarithmic (such as volume controls).

You must make certain compromises on a computer screen because the controls lack physical consistency. A flat rotary knob on a computer screen is difficult to manipulate. A sliding pot might work better. This control has a cursor you can move either vertically or horizontally. Chapter 4 described the *Cursor* class, which provides both precise and delicate control. This section describes several kinds of Pots. Figure 5.3 shows their genealogy.

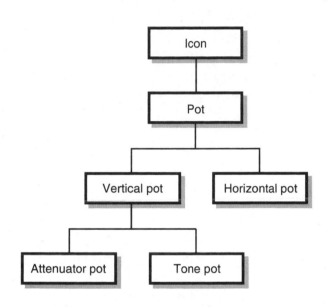

Fig. 5.3. The genealogy of potentiometers.

Attenuators are used in electronics to reduce—or attenuate—signals. Class AttenuatorPot is a specialized potentiometer designed to reduce the value of a floating-point variable between 0 and 102 decibels (dB). The class *TonePot* is a specialization of potentiometers that can be used by an application program to reduce or increase the level of a variable. The adjustment level allowed by a *TonePot* is between -20 dB and 20 dB.

A tone control set to 0 dB is said to be "flat," because it does not cut or boost any particular frequency. You derive any other vertical or horizontal pot by following the coding examples. The following listings, which are excerpted from files *pot.hpp* and *pot.cpp*, show the coding for class *Pot* and its siblings. You can see most of the *Pot* classes described by running the demo program on the companion disk and selecting page *Recorder*.

Listing 5.1. The declaration for class Pot.

```
class Pot: public Icon {

public:

    friend class Cursor;

    char legend [MAX_LEGEND_LENGTH + 1];
    ShadedBox* pot_box;
    Cursor* cursor;
    float* pot_setting;
    void (*activation_function)();
    float minimum, maximum;
    char* units;

    COLOR_TYPE shade_color;
    COLOR_TYPE border_color;
    COLOR_TYPE legend_color;
    COLOR_TYPE legend_backdrop_color;
    COLOR_TYPE inactive_color;
    COLOR_TYPE active_color;
    COLOR_TYPE fill_color;

    Pot(int, int, int, int,
        int, int, int, int,
        float, float, char*,
        int, int,
        char*, float*, void (*) (),
        COLOR_TYPE, COLOR_TYPE, COLOR_TYPE,
        COLOR_TYPE, COLOR_TYPE);
    virtual void Display();
    void Setting(float value);
    float Setting()              {return *pot_setting;}
    virtual void SettingDisplay();
    virtual ~Pot();
};


#define VERTICAL_POT_WIDTH 80
#define VERTICAL_POT_HEIGHT 100
#define VERTICAL_POT_CURSOR_WIDTH (VERTICAL_POT_WIDTH -
5)
#define VERTICAL_POT_CURSOR_HEIGHT 10

class VerticalPot: public Pot {

public:

    VerticalPot(int x, int y,
            float min, float max, char* units,
            char* name, float* value, void (*)() );
```

```
        virtual void SettingDisplay() {Pot::SettingDisplay();}
};


class AttenuatorPot: public VerticalPot {

public:

        AttenuatorPot(int x, int y, char* l, float* v,
                        void (*)() );
};



#define TONE_MIN_LEVEL (-20)
#define TONE_MAX_LEVEL (20)

class ToneLevelPot: public VerticalPot {

public:

        ToneLevelPot(int x, int y, char* l, float* v,
                        void (*) () );
};


#define HORIZONTAL_POT_WIDTH 100
#define HORIZONTAL_POT_HEIGHT 60
#define HORIZONTAL_POT_CURSOR_HEIGHT \
     (HORIZONTAL_POT_HEIGHT - (2 * POT_LEGEND_HEIGHT) - 5)
#define HORIZONTAL_POT_CURSOR_WIDTH 10

class HorizontalPot: public Pot {

public:

        HorizontalPot(int x, int y,
                 float min, float max, char* units,
                 char* name, float* value, void (*)() );

     virtual void SettingDisplay() {Pot::SettingDisplay();}
};



#endif
```

Listing 5.2. The implementation of class Pot.

```
#include "pot.hpp"

Pot::Pot(int x, int y, int width, int height,
        int min_x, int min_y, int max_x, int max_y,
        float min_cursor, float max_cursor, char* pot_units,
        int cursor_width, int cursor_height,
        char* name, float* initial_setting,
        void (*activate)(),
        COLOR_TYPE shade_clr, COLOR_TYPE border_clr,
        COLOR_TYPE inactive_clr, COLOR_TYPE active_clr,
        COLOR_TYPE legend_clr) :

        Icon(x, y, x + width, y + height)
{
    minimum = min_cursor;
    maximum = max_cursor;
    units = pot_units;

    // make a copy of the reference variable
    // and the activation function, which will
    // be invoked when the pot is used
    strncpy(legend, name, size of(legend) - 1);
    pot_setting = initial_setting;
    activation_function = activate;

    shade_color = shade_clr;
    border_color = border_clr;
    legend_color = legend_clr;
    fill_color = legend_backdrop_color =
            inactive_color = inactive_clr;
    active_color = active_clr;

    pot_box = new ShadedBox(x1, y1,
                    x2 - x1,
                    y2 - y1,
                    shade_color,
                    border_color,
                    fill_color);

    cursor = new Cursor(this, cursor_width, cursor_height,
                    min_x, min_y,
                    max_x, max_y,
                    fill_color);
}

void Pot::Display()
{
```

```
        pot_box->Display();

        // subdivide pot into areas
        BOX_TYPE box;
        box.x1 = x1 + 1;
        box.y1 = y1 + POT_LEGEND_HEIGHT + 1;
        box.x2 = x2 - 2;
        box.y2 = y2 - POT_LEGEND_HEIGHT - 2;
        GraphicsHandler->DrawBox(border_color,
                                 SOLID_LINE, &box);

        // center title on pot
        box.x1 = x1 + 1;
        box.y1 = y1;
        box.x2 = x2 - 2;
        box.y2 = y1 + POT_LEGEND_HEIGHT;
        Legend pot_legend;
        pot_legend.Center(&box, legend_color, legend);

        // display the cursor controls
        cursor->Display();
        SettingDisplay();
}


void Pot::Setting(float value)
{
        // update the pot s setting variable
        *pot_setting = value;

        // invoke the application program to
        // handle the pot
        if (activation_function)
          (*activation_function)();
}

void Pot::SettingDisplay()
{
        // erase previous string
        BOX_TYPE box;
        box.x1 = x1 + 3;
        box.y1 = y2 - POT_LEGEND_HEIGHT;
        box.x2 = x2 - 4;
        box.y2 = y2 - 6;
        GraphicsHandler->FillBox(legend_backdrop_color, &box);

        // convert the setting from range (0..1) to the proper
            // range for this pot
            float displayed_value = \
                *pot_setting * (maximum - minimum) + minimum;
```

Listing 5.2 Continues

Listing 5.2 Continued

```
        // display the new setting, centered
        char text [40];
        sprintf(text, "%.1f %s", displayed_value, units);
        Legend pot_setting;
        pot_setting.Center(&box, legend_color, text);
}

Pot::~Pot()
{
    delete pot_box;
    delete cursor;
}


VerticalPot::VerticalPot(int x, int y,
                float min, float max, char* units,
                char* name, float* value,
                void (*activate)() ) :

        Pot(x, y,
        VERTICAL_POT_WIDTH, VERTICAL_POT_HEIGHT,
        x + 2,
        y + POT_LEGEND_HEIGHT + 2,
        x + 2,
        y + VERTICAL_POT_HEIGHT - POT_LEGEND_HEIGHT - \
        3 - VERTICAL_POT_CURSOR_HEIGHT,
        min, max, units,
        VERTICAL_POT_CURSOR_WIDTH,
        VERTICAL_POT_CURSOR_HEIGHT,
        name, value, activate,
        BLACK,
        BRIGHT_GREEN,
        BRIGHT_BLUE,
        BRIGHT_CYAN,
        WHITE)
{}


AttenuatorPot::AttenuatorPot(int x, int y, char* l,
                float* v, void (*f)() ) :
        VerticalPot(x, y, -102, 0, "dB", l, v, f)
{}


ToneLevelPot::ToneLevelPot(int x, int y, char* l,
                float* v, void (*f)() ) :

        VerticalPot(x, y, TONE_MIN_LEVEL,
                TONE_MAX_LEVEL, "dB", l, v, f)
    {}
```

```
HorizontalPot::HorizontalPot(int x, int y,
             float min, float max, char* units,
             char* name, float* value,
             void (*activate)() ) :

     Pot(x, y,
     HORIZONTAL_POT_WIDTH, HORIZONTAL_POT_HEIGHT,
     x + 2,
     y + POT_LEGEND_HEIGHT + 2,
     x + HORIZONTAL_POT_WIDTH - \
         HORIZONTAL_POT_CURSOR_WIDTH - 3,
     y + POT_LEGEND_HEIGHT + 2,
     min, max, units,
     HORIZONTAL_POT_CURSOR_WIDTH,
     HORIZONTAL_POT_CURSOR_HEIGHT,
     name, value, activate,
     BLACK,
     BRIGHT_GREEN,
     BRIGHT_BLUE,
     BRIGHT_CYAN,
     WHITE)
  {}
```

Function Descriptions

Pot::Pot

The class constructor registers the basic variables, such as the limits of the cursor excursion, the object's colors, and the legend. It also creates two dynamically allocated objects: a shaded box, which serves as a background for the control, and the mobile cursor.

Pot::Display

This function paints the potentiometer on the screen. First it displays a shaded box, and then it divides the box into a top and a bottom part. The parts show a legend and a setting value.

Pot::Setting

This function updates the setting of the pot to a certain value. Moving the cursor of a pot results in a change of setting. If the application program has defined a function to handle changes, it is invoked.

Pot::SettingDisplay

This function computes the value of a pot's setting through the position of its cursor. It then shows the new setting in the top area of the pot box, centered and with appropriate units.

Pot::~Pot

The destructor reclaims the dynamically allocated objects and then removes itself from the display list (via the base class destructor).

VerticalPot::VerticalPot

These pots' cursors slide vertically. Volume controls, level adjustments, and temperature controls frequently use such cursors. No other functions are necessary for generic vertical pots, because all the functionality is inherited from class *Pot*.

AttenuatorPot::AttenuatorPot

This is the only function necessary to provide full functionality to a generic attenuator. All the other behaviors come without change from class *VerticalPot*. Here, an attenuator is a pot with a value of attenuation ranging from 0 to -102 decibels.

ToneLevelPot::ToneLevelPot

This type of control sets the treble and bass of an audio signal. Its structure is similar to an attenuator, except for the range allowed (between +20 and

-20 dB). This class could easily override any of the base class's parameters, such as color, size, or shape.

HorizontalPot::HorizontalPot

These pots' cursors slide horizontally. Stereo balance controls and tuning controls in a radio use horizontal pots. Like their vertical counterparts, they have standard attributes such as shape, size, and color, but these are all easily overridden in derived classes. Generic horizontal pots need no other functions, because all the functionality comes from class *Pot*.

The Selector Class

You often must select a setting from a given set of options on a control panel. Potentiometers provide a smooth, continuous range of selection, but sometimes only discrete settings are possible or desirable. Consider the control panel for an elevator, shown in figure 5.4. Integer numbers should be available as a selection.

The *Selector* class solves this problem and makes the creation of both vertical (as shown in figure 5.4) and horizontal possible. The selectors described here have an unusual characteristic: their size is variable. All other objects in this book have a size determined at compile time. To use this approach for selectors would entail a separate class for selectors with two buttons, three buttons, and so on. It's simpler to use a single class for all cases, determining dynamically the number of buttons. The above implementation of class *Selector* allows you to create controls with up to eight buttons. If you need more than eight, you need to modify the macro MAX_SELECTOR_BUTTONS and recompile the class. Figure 5.5 shows the genealogy of selectors.

Selector objects' layouts are similar to *Pots*; they use a shaded box as the background and a bottom area for the legend. The top part is where the control buttons show up. Clicking (or touching) a control button makes it active. All other buttons become inactive. Only one button can be active at any given time. Listing 5.3 shows the header file for class *Selector*.

Fig. 5.4. A vertical selector used in an elevator display panel.

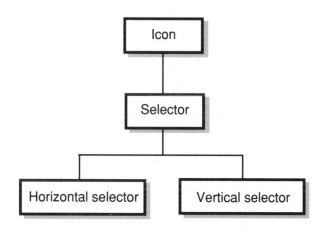

Fig. 5.5. The genealogy of class Selector.

Listing 5.3. The header file for class Selector and its siblings.

```
#ifndef SELECTORHPP
#define SELECTORHPP

#include <string.h>

#include "icon.hpp"
#include "box.hpp"
#include "limit.hpp"
```

```
#include "graphics.hpp"
#include "database.hpp"
#include "legend.hpp"

#define SELECTOR_BUTTON_WIDTH 60
#define SELECTOR_BUTTON_HEIGHT 30
#define SELECTOR_LEFT_MARGIN 10
#define SELECTOR_RIGHT_MARGIN 10
#define SELECTOR_TOP_MARGIN 3
#define SELECTOR_BOTTOM_MARGIN 3
#define SELECTOR_LEGEND_HEIGHT 13

#define MAX_SELECTOR_BUTTONS 8

// types of selectors
#define VERTICAL_SELECTOR 0
#define HORIZONTAL_SELECTOR 1

class Selector: public Icon {

    friend class Button;
    int x1, y1, x2, y2;
    char selector_legend [MAX_LEGEND_LENGTH + 1];
    char *button_legend [MAX_SELECTOR_BUTTONS];
    int number_of_buttons;
    ShadedBox* selector_box;

protected:

    int *button_selected;
    Button* button [MAX_SELECTOR_BUTTONS];
    void (*activation_function)();

    COLOR_TYPE shade_color;
    COLOR_TYPE border_color;
    COLOR_TYPE fill_color;
    COLOR_TYPE inactive_color;
    COLOR_TYPE active_color;
    COLOR_TYPE legend_color;

public:

    Selector(int, int, int, char*, int*, void (*)(),
        char* = 0,
        char* = 0,
        char* = 0,
        char* = 0,
        char* = 0,
        char* = 0,
        char* = 0,
        char* = 0);
```

Listing 5.3 Continues

109

Listing 5.3 Continued

```
    void Display();
    virtual void Select(int button);
    virtual void Update() {}
    virtual void LeftButtonPressed() {}
    virtual void LeftButtonReleased() {}
    virtual ~Selector();
};

class Button: public Icon {

    int x1, y1, x2, y2;
    Selector* parent_selector;
    int button_number;
    char legend [MAX_LEGEND_LENGTH + 1];
    Box* box;

    COLOR_TYPE inactive_color;
    COLOR_TYPE active_color;
    COLOR_TYPE border_color;
    COLOR_TYPE fill_color;
    COLOR_TYPE legend_color;
    COLOR_TYPE legend_backdrop_color;

public:

    Button(Selector*, int, int, int, int, int, char*,
      COLOR_TYPE, COLOR_TYPE, COLOR_TYPE, COLOR_TYPE);
    void Display();
    void Color(COLOR_TYPE);
    void Highlight();
    void UnHighlight();
    void SetLegend(char* string) {
      strncpy(legend, string, size of(legend) );}
    void LeftButtonPressed();
    virtual ~Button();
};


class HorizontalSelector: public Selector {

public:

    HorizontalSelector(int bx, int by,
        char *selector_title,
        int *initial_selection,
        void (*function)(),
        char *button1_title,
        char* = 0,
        char* = 0,
        char* = 0,
```

```
                    char* = 0,
                    char* = 0,
                    char* = 0,
                    char* = 0);
        virtual void Select(int button) {
          Selector::Select(button);}
        virtual void Update() {}
        virtual void LeftButtonPressed() {}
        virtual void LeftButtonReleased() {}
};

class VerticalSelector: public Selector {

public:

        VerticalSelector(
                int bx, int by,
                char *selector_title,
                int *initial_selection,
                void (*function)(),
                char *button1_title,
                char* = 0,
                char* = 0,
                char* = 0,
                char* = 0,
                char* = 0,
                char* = 0,
                char* = 0);
        virtual void Select(int button) {
          Selector::Select(button);}
        virtual void Update() {}
        virtual void LeftButtonPressed() {}
        virtual void LeftButtonReleased() {}
};

#endif
```

Class *Button* is declared a **friend** in *Selector*, but not because it needs access to the internals of *Selector*. The fact is, the *Selector* declares an array of pointers to *Button* objects, but this isn't allowed unless the *Button* identifier has been introduced into scope. An incomplete class declaration suffices as a forward reference, but the **friend** declaration can also be used to bring an identifier into scope.

Class *Selector* is designed to be extended. To this end it has many virtual member functions, allowing most of its methods to be overridden. The following listings show the implementation of class *Selector*.

Listing 5.4. The implementation of class Selector *and its siblings.*

```
#include "selector.hpp"

Selector::Selector(int x, int y, int type,
            char *selector_title,
            int *initial_selection,
            void (*function)(),
            char *button1_title,
            char *button2_title,
            char *button3_title,
            char *button4_title,
            char *button5_title,
            char *button6_title,
            char *button7_title,
            char *button8_title) :

      Icon(x, y, x, y)      // we'll set x2, y2 later

{
      button_legend [0] = button1_title;
      button_legend [1] = button2_title;
      button_legend [2] = button3_title;
      button_legend [3] = button4_title;
      button_legend [4] = button5_title;
      button_legend [5] = button6_title;
      button_legend [6] = button7_title;
      button_legend [7] = button8_title;

      // find out how many buttons the selector has
      number_of_buttons = 0;
      for (int i = 0; i < MAX_SELECTOR_BUTTONS; i++) {
        if (button_legend [i])
          number_of_buttons++;
        else
          break;
      }

      // keep a copy of the title and activation function
      strncpy(selector_legend,
          selector_title,
          MAX_LEGEND_LENGTH);
      activation_function = function;
      button_selected = initial_selection;

      shade_color = BLACK;
      border_color = WHITE;
      fill_color = GRAY;
      inactive_color = CYAN;
      active_color = BRIGHT_CYAN;
      legend_color = BLACK;
```

```
        int width, height;
        if (type == VERTICAL_SELECTOR) {

          // vertically displayed buttons
          width = SELECTOR_BUTTON_WIDTH + \
                  SELECTOR_LEFT_MARGIN + \
                  SELECTOR_RIGHT_MARGIN;

          height = number_of_buttons * SELECTOR_BUTTON_HEIGHT +
\
                  SELECTOR_TOP_MARGIN + \
                  SELECTOR_LEGEND_HEIGHT + \
                  SELECTOR_BOTTOM_MARGIN;
        }

        else {

          // horizontally displayed buttons
          width = number_of_buttons * SELECTOR_BUTTON_WIDTH + \
                  SELECTOR_LEFT_MARGIN + \
                  SELECTOR_RIGHT_MARGIN;

          height = SELECTOR_BUTTON_HEIGHT + \
                  SELECTOR_TOP_MARGIN + \
                  SELECTOR_LEGEND_HEIGHT + \
                  SELECTOR_BOTTOM_MARGIN;
        }

        x1 = x;
        y1 = y;
        x2 = x1 + width;
        y2 = y1 + height;

        // dynamically update width of Icon
        Icon::x2 = x2;
        Icon::y2 = y2;

        selector_box = new ShadedBox(x1, y1,
                            width, height,
                            shade_color,
                            border_color,
                            fill_color);

        for (i = 0; i < number_of_buttons; i++) {
          if (type == VERTICAL_SELECTOR) {
            // show buttons vertically
            button [i] = new Button(this, i,
              x1 + SELECTOR_LEFT_MARGIN,
              y2 - SELECTOR_TOP_MARGIN - \
```

Listing 5.4 Continues

113

Listing 5.4 Continued

```
                (i + 1) * SELECTOR_BUTTON_HEIGHT,
            SELECTOR_BUTTON_WIDTH,
            SELECTOR_BUTTON_HEIGHT,
            button_legend [i],
            shade_color,
            inactive_color,
            active_color,
            BLACK);
      }
      else {
        // show buttons horizontally
        button [i] = new Button(this, i,
                x1 + SELECTOR_LEFT_MARGIN + \
                  i * SELECTOR_BUTTON_WIDTH,
                y1 + SELECTOR_LEGEND_HEIGHT +
                  SELECTOR_TOP_MARGIN,
                SELECTOR_BUTTON_WIDTH,
                SELECTOR_BUTTON_HEIGHT,
                button_legend [i],
                shade_color,
                inactive_color,
                active_color,
                BLACK);
      }
    }
}


void Selector::Display()
{
    selector_box->Display();
    for (int i = 0; i < number_of_buttons; i++) {
      if (i == *button_selected)
        button [i]->Highlight();
      else
        button [i]->Display();
    }

    // partition off the legend area
    BOX_TYPE line;
    line.x1 = x1 + 2;
    line.y1 = y1 + SELECTOR_LEGEND_HEIGHT + 2;
    line.x2 = x2 - 2;
    line.y2 = line.y1;
    GraphicsHandler->DrawLine(border_color,
                    SOLID_LINE,
                    &line);
```

```
        // display the selector legend
        BOX_TYPE box;
        box.x1 = x1;
        box.y1 = y1 + 2;
        box.x2 = x2;
        box.y2 = y1 + SELECTOR_LEGEND_HEIGHT;
        Legend title_legend;
        title_legend.Center(&box,
                        legend_color,
                        selector_legend);
}


void Selector::Select(int selection)
{
        // abort if invalid selections attempted
        if (selection >= number_of_buttons) return;
        if (selection < 0) return;

        // capture the selection
        *button_selected = selection;

        // turn on the selection; turn off everything
        // else
        for (int i = 0; i < number_of_buttons; i++) {
          if (i == selection)
              button [i]->Color(active_color);
            else
              button [i]->Color(inactive_color);
          button [i]->Display();
        }
        // invoke the activation function so that the
        // application program can execute the command
        if (activation_function)
          (*activation_function)();
}


Selector::~Selector()
{
        delete selector_box;

        for (int i = 0; i < number_of_buttons; i++)
          delete button [i];
}


Button::Button(Selector* parent, int number,
                int cx, int cy,
                int width, int height,
                char* button_legend,
```

Listing 5.4 Continues

Listing 5.4 Continued

```
                        COLOR_TYPE border_clr,
                        COLOR_TYPE inactive_clr,
                        COLOR_TYPE active_clr,
                        COLOR_TYPE legend_clr) :
    Icon(cx + 1, cy + 1,
        cx + width - 1, cy + height - 1)
{
    x1 = cx + 1;
    y1 = cy + 1;
    x2 = x1 + width - 2;
    y2 = y1 + height - 2;
    parent_selector = parent;
    SetLegend(button_legend);
    button_number = number;
    border_color = border_clr;
    active_color = active_clr;
    inactive_color = inactive_clr;
    fill_color = inactive_color;
    legend_color = legend_clr;
    box = new Box(x1, y1, x2 - x1, y2 - y1,
                border_color,
                fill_color);
}

void Button::Display()
{

    box->Display();

    // display the switch legend
    BOX_TYPE box;
    box.x1 = x1;
    box.y1 = y1;
    box.x2 = x2;
    box.y2 = y2;
    Legend title_legend;
    title_legend.Center(&box, legend_color, legend);
}

void Button::Color(COLOR_TYPE color)
{
    fill_color = color;
    box->Color(fill_color);
}

void Button::Highlight()
{
```

```
        fill_color = active_color;
        box->Color(fill_color);
        Display();
}

void Button::UnHighlight()
{
        fill_color = inactive_color;
        box->Color(fill_color);
        Display();
}

void Button::LeftButtonPressed()
{
        parent_selector->Select(button_number);
}


Button::~Button()
{
        delete box;
}



HorizontalSelector::HorizontalSelector(int bx, int by,
            char *selector_title,
            int *initial_selection,
            void (*function)(),
            char *button1_title,
            char *button2_title,
            char *button3_title,
            char *button4_title,
            char *button5_title,
            char *button6_title,
            char *button7_title,
            char *button8_title) :

        Selector(bx, by, HORIZONTAL_SELECTOR,
        selector_title, initial_selection,
        function,
        button1_title,
        button2_title,
        button3_title,
        button4_title,
        button5_title,
        button6_title,
        button7_title,
        button8_title)
{}
```

Listing 5.4 Continues

Listing 5.4 Continued

```
VerticalSelector::VerticalSelector(
        int bx, int by,
        char *selector_title,
        int *initial_selection,
        void (*function)(),
            char *button1_title,
            char *button2_title,
            char *button3_title,
            char *button4_title,
            char *button5_title,
            char *button6_title,
            char *button7_title,
            char *button8_title) :

        Selector(bx, by, VERTICAL_SELECTOR,
        selector_title, initial_selection,
        function,
        button1_title,
        button2_title,
        button3_title,
        button4_title,
        button5_title,
        button6_title,
        button7_title,
        button8_title)
    {}
```

Function Descriptions

Selector::Selector

The class constructor is utilized to construct both vertical and horizontal selectors. The function counts the number of strings passed to it, to determine the number of child buttons to create. To compute the final size of the selector object, the constructor considers the type of selector (vertical or horizontal) and the number of buttons needed. A shaded box is created as a backdrop, and then the buttons are added. The constructor does not paint anything on the screen, it just creates the necessary objects.

Selector::Display

This function shows the entire selector object. First it shows the background shaded box, and then each of the buttons on top of it. The button set to the active state (if any) will show up as a highlighted object. The selector buttons are partitioned off from the selector's name. As usual, the *Legend* object centers the name in the bottom area.

Selector::Select

Clicking or touching one of the child buttons invokes this virtual function. It is the default *Select* function for derived classes, unless overridden. The selector deactivates all other buttons and activates the one selected. The button is then highlighted, and the application program's handler function is invoked.

Selector::~Selector

The class destructor returns the dynamically allocated objects to the free list and removes itself from the display list via the base-class destructor. This function does not repaint the screen to restore it to a previous state.

Button::Button

Do not confuse these buttons with the ones used in push buttons. Class *Button* should behave as a child because it notifies its parent when it is selected. In addition, child status requires an identifier so each button can identify itself to the parent. For simplicity's sake, the buttons in selectors are numbered sequentially. The constructor function saves all the state variables for the button and creates a box to use as a backdrop for the button. The constructor does not modify the screen.

Button::Display

This function displays the box around the button and centers the button title in it. The color saved in the variable *fill_color* paints the box. The Highlight and UnHighlight functions manipulate *fill_color*.

Button::Color

This function sets the fill color to a new value. The color remains set until changed explicitly. Changing the color of a button does not automatically update the screen.

Button::Highlight

This function makes the color of the button brighter than normal. The function does update the screen. Invoke Button::Display to repaint the object.

Button::UnHighlight

This function works likes its counterpart Highlight and restores the button's color to its normal inactive state. The screen is updated.

Button::LeftButtonPressed

Clicking on a button calls this function. The action sends a message to the parent selector to deactivate all other buttons. The entire selector is then repainted.

Button::~Button

The destructor merely relinquishes the memory used for the background box and then cleans up the display list via the base-class destructor. The above implementation of class *Selector* allows you to create controls with up to eight buttons. If you need more than eight, you'll have to modify the macro MAX_SELECTOR_BUTTONS and recompile the class. Figure 5.5 shows the genealogy of selectors.

HorizontalSelector::HorizontalSelector

This constructor's sole role is to pass parameters to the base class *Selector*, which then does all the work. The screen is not updated.

VerticalSelector::VerticalSelector

This constructor is like the previous one except for the values passed to the base class.

6

The Page Class

As you saw in Chapter 3, the overall screen area comprises two main parts: the work area and the page-selector area. The work area displays the application-dependent pages. The page selector is a special control for selecting pages. Selecting a page erases the previous one and replaces it with the new one.

You should consider everything shown in the screen work area as part of a page. Think of pages on the screen as pages in a book; the user can utilize special page-selector buttons on the side of the screen to peruse the pages. Organizing data into pages is important when designing a practical user interface.

First is the consideration of the user's information bandwidth, which indicates how much data can be dealt with at one time. Giving the user too much information usually results in poor communication. Important things, such as an alarm condition or a critical gauge reading, can be difficult to spot.

The second consideration is presenting information so related items show up together. This technique provides the user with easy cross-referencing and appropriate mental associations. Any feature that reinforces a user's mental model of the system makes the system easier to master.

The class *Page* is not built from scratch. Because it is part of the screen, it needs some extra machinery from the root class *Icon*. Figure 6.1 shows the genealogy of class *Page*.

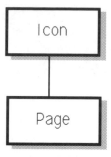

Fig. 6.1. The simple genealogy of class Page.

As classes go, *Page* is a simple one. In general, each class in a complex system should inherit as much as possible and contribute only the minimum necessary. This policy enhances reusability and leads to lower replication of functions across the hierarchy, one measure of the efficiency of a system's code.

The most basic page is a blank one, which occupies the central area of the screen. I refer to this space as the *work area*. Each page displays its title at the top. This top area is also part of a page object.

You can make many additions and variations to the basic layout of a page. You might want to reserve a space in a corner for a company logo or apply special fixed controls, such as a help button or the date, that appear on every page. This book's code uses a simple layout with a work area and a series of controls for selecting pages. Figure 6.2 shows how the demo program on the companion disk appears before you select a page. The page selector is on the right side of the screen.

Real pages have additional controls and icons that deal with the application program. The base class *Page* doesn't support the various objects placed on the application page because it doesn't know they exist. Each specific page is a separate derived class responsible for handling the added features. Class inheritance thus saves considerable time when building custom pages. Listings 6.1 and 6.2 show the header and source code for class *Page*.

Fig. 6.2. An empty page with a page selector.

Listing 6.1. The header file for class Page.

```
#ifndef PAGEHPP
#define PAGEHPP
#include "icon.hpp"
#include "descrip.hpp"
#include "screen.hpp"

class Page : public Icon {

     Description* title; // title of the page

public:

     Page(char*);
     virtual void Display();
     virtual ~Page();
};

#endif
```

Listing 6.2. The implementation of class Page.

```
#include "page.hpp"

Page::Page(char* page_title) : Icon(-1, -1, -1, -1)
{
     title = new Description (SCREEN_TITLE_X1,
                    SCREEN_TITLE_Y1,
                    SCREEN_TITLE_X2,
                    SCREEN_TITLE_Y2,
                    YELLOW, GRAY, BLUE);

     title->SetText(page_title);
}


void Page::Display()
{
     title->Display();
}


Page::~Page()
{
     delete title;
}
```

Function Descriptions

Page::Page

The class constructor's main function is to invoke its base class *Icon* with fictitious offscreen coordinates. Now the display list has an icon with coordinates you'll never select with a mouse event, because clicking a mouse provides no defined behavior for objects of class *Page*. Other applications can elect to change this concept. For example, you could scroll or reposition a page with the mouse. The class would need to override the virtual mouse-processing functions in class *Icon*, as class *Cursor* does.

The only thing the constructor does itself is to create an object of class *Description*, which reserves an area of the screen for the page title. The title is then passed to *Description* for subsequent use. After the constructor terminates, the page object no longer knows the page title, and relies on the subclass *Description* to display it.

Page::Display

This function displays the page title at the top of the screen, centered inside a box. all the parameters for the title, including color, location, and text, are set once and for all by the page constructor and passed on to class *Description*. In fact, class *Page* keeps no record of details regarding its title. Such data hiding makes a system easier to maintain.

Page::~Page

This function deletes the title object and removes itself from the display list (via the base class destructor).

Building a Custom Page

All the page functions described so far provide only a framework for writing a real application page such as the one shown in figure 6.3. This section shows how to derive a custom page class that could represent a real-life situation. In doing so, you will see how easy it is to design and develop control pages for your own applications.

Assume that you are designing a computerized system for a nuclear-reactor control room. One page shows the temperature reading for a certain area of the plant's cooling system. A special readout indicates when a temperature has gone critical. You need controls to acknowledge these alarms and decide to lay the page out, as figure 6.3 shows.

The page needs three different types of special icons: temperature bar graphs, alarm panels, and acknowledge buttons. For now the focus is on how these basic building blocks fit into the page structure. Later chapters will go into the details of creating objects similar to the ones in this example.

Assume that the three controls have the following class names:

- TemperatureBarGraph

- AlarmPanel

- AcknowledgeButton

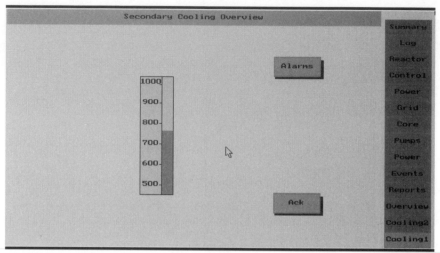

Fig. 6.3. The temperature control page.

These objects, in turn, contain an opportune genealogy stemming from the base class *Icon*. The new page class is *TemperaturePage*. Its header file is *temppage.hpp*, as shown in listing 6.3.

Listing 6.3. The header file for class TemperaturePage.

```
#ifndef TEMPERATURE_PAGE_HPP
#define TEMPERATURE_PAGE_HPP

#include "page.hpp"
#include "screen.hpp"
#include "tempbar.hpp"
#include "alarm.hpp"
#include "ackbutton.hpp"

class TemperaturePage: public Page {

    TemperatureBarGraph*  temperature;
    AlarmPanel*           alarm;
    AcknowledgeButton*    acknowledge;

public:

    TemperaturePage();
    void Display();
    ~TemperaturePage();
};

void OpenTemperaturePage();
#endif
```

The first *#ifndef* and *#define* statements constitute the usual multiple-inclusion trap. Next come the *#includes* for the classes *TemperaturePage* uses. Inside the class definition are pointers to the actual control icons managed by *TemperaturePage* itself.

Near the end of file *temppage.hpp* is the declaration

```
void OpenTemperaturePage();
```

Oddly enough, the declaration occurs *outside* the class *TemperaturePage*; thus, the function is not part of the class. There's a good reason for this. OpenTemperaturePage provides a generic solution to the problem of creating arbitrary application-specific pages through a consistent paging mechanism. Although Page selectors are dealt with in the following chapter, the following details clarify the need for OpenTemperaturePage.

The page selector is an array of buttons. Each button has a customizable feature, known as its activation function, which normally invokes a function inside the application program. For page-selector buttons, the activation function must create and display an entire application page, with all its controls and readouts. The function OpenTemperaturePage is designed to be the activation function for a page selector button. Each application page has a similar function, and all the application pages are handled via the global structure *Pages*, in the file *database.cpp*. This structure is used by the page-selector class. Each entry contains the legend of a selector button and the associated application function. Chapter 7 illustrates the paging mechanism in detail.

Listing 6.4 is for file *temppage.cpp*. The constructor's basic operation is passing the page title to the base class, which in turn implements the entire page machinery. Only the creation of the specific controls used is new. The member function *Display* paints those controls on the screen, but it first invokes the base class to display itself. It displays the title along with anything else added to class *Page*. The destructor is also as simple as possible, performing only the deletion of the controls created on top of the basic page.

The page selector buttons invoke the function *OpenTemperaturePage*. It creates an instance of class *TemperaturePage*, attaches it to the screen as the icon in the work area, and displays it. Every derived page needs a similar *hook* function for a simple call to perform the create-and-display duties.

Listing 6.4. The implementation for class TemperaturePage.

```
#include "temppage.hpp"

TemperaturePage::TemperaturePage() :
     Page("Secondary Cooling Overview")
{
     temperature = new TemperatureBarGraph(300, 200,
                         "Temperature",
                         &TemperatureReading);

     alarm = new AlarmPanel(400, 250,
                         "Temperature Alarm",
                         &TemperatureAlarm);

     acknowledge = new AcknowledgeButton(300, 20,
                         "Acknowledge",
                         &AcknowledgeState);
}

void TemperaturePage::Display()
{
     Page::Display();
     temperature->Display();
     alarm->Display();
     acknowledge->Display();
}

TemperaturePage::~TemperaturePage()
{
     // destroy all objects on the screen
     delete temperature;
     delete alarm;
     delete acknowledge;
}

void OpenTemperaturePage()
{
     // get next page ready
     TemperaturePage* new_page = new TemperaturePage();
     // and display it
     CurrentScreen->NewWorkArea(new_page);
     CurrentScreen->DisplayWorkArea();
}
```

The class *TemperaturePage* is just an example of the types of functions that need to be provided in generic application-specific pages. There must always be a constructor and destructor. In addition you need functions equivalent to *Display* and *OpenTemperaturePage*. Mouse clicks may even be supported at the page level as well. To do this you must modify the coordinates passed by the *Page* constructor to the base class *Icon*. Currently the coordinates (-1, -1) are used, but they should be changed to indicate the actual coordinates of the work area of the screen.

The code in listing 6.4 is to be used as a template. all the pages shown in the demo program follow this scheme. It is important that the class destructor eliminate ALL the objects used in the class. The page class is easily extensible and may be used over and over again by the widest rangest of applications.

7

The PageSelector Class

Chapter 3 described the working-area and the page-selector areas of the screen. The many control icons of the GUI are subdivided into pages. the screen displays these pages in the working area, one page at a time.

To get conveniently to controls not shown on the current page, you could flip through the various pages of the interface as you would a book. Better yet, you could use a direct-access method to go directly to specific pages. The class *PageSelector* satisfies this need, displaying a vertical array of buttons along the side of the screen. Clicking them takes you directly to the corresponding page.

The page selector is different from previous controls. It belongs to the GUI and not to the underlying application program. In fact, the application program shouldn't even need to know what pages are. There is no direct connection between a page selector and code in the application. The control variable used in the page selector is not accessible by the application. The page selector should be displayed in such a way as to not interfere with the rest of the system, and should be kept out of the working area of the screen. Page selectors are often placed along the lower or right edges of the screen. This is practical for right-handed people, especially when using a touch-sensitive screen, because they can press buttons without obscuring the rest of the screen. For mouse users, the placement of the page selector is usually not critical. A well-designed GUI should allow the user to move the page selector anywhere on the screen. Figure 7.1 shows the general layout for the page-selector icon.

Conceptually, a page selector is similar to the *VerticalSelector* presented earlier, but here are a few of the important differences:

1. Pressing a button does not activate the application program.

2. No title appears on a page selector (as implemented here).

3. The page selector must create and display entire pages, not single icons.

Such differences suggest implementing a separate class not derived from *VerticalSelector*. This book uses the simple inheritance tree shown in figure 7.2.Fig. 7.1.

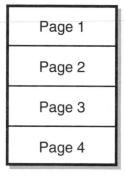

Fig. 7.1. The general layout for a page selector.

Pages can be organized in a variety of ways. They can be considered to be a linear sequence, without any sense of hierarchy. They can be grouped into the equivalent of book chapters, or they can be organized into complex multilevel trees. The page organization used by a GUI depends on the type and number of pages required. Using a hierarchical approach, the first page shown in a GUI would be the main page, and the page buttons would allow you to navigate through a sequence of pages that could be quite involved. For the code in this book, I have kept things simple: pages are essentially unstructured, and the same page buttons are displayed on all page selections.

The class *PageSelector* has an implementation different from the other classes shown in this book: it makes use of a global variable expected to contain certain necessary initialization data. This variable is actually an array called *Pages*, kept in the file *database.cpp*. As stated earlier, *PageSelector* belongs to the GUI rather than to the application program, and yet it manipulates application-specific pages. In other words, *PageSelector* has access to the application pages, without being part of the application. Here the array *Pages* comes into play. Each application program sets up *Pages* differently. The demo program on the companion disk initializes *Pages* as follows:

```
typedef struct PAGE_BUTTON_DEFINITION {
  char descriptor [MAX_LEGEND_LENGTH + 1];
  void (*activation_function)();
} PAGE_BUTTON_DEFINITION;

PAGE_BUTTON_DEFINITION Pages [MAX_PAGE_BUTTON] = {
  "Recorder",  OpenRecorderPage,
  "Piano",   OpenPianoPage,
  "PingPong",     OpenBallPage,
  "Tanks",   OpenVatPage,
  "Clocks",  OpenClockPage,
  "Games",   OpenGamePage,
   0,        0,
};
```

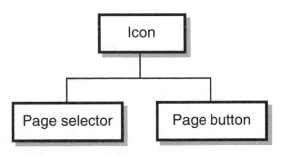

Fig. 7.2. The genealogy of class PageSelector and its child controls.

As you can see, each line of the array contains two entries: the first is the label to be written on a page-selector button; the second is the function to be invoked when you click that button. This function is referred to as an *activation function*. The purpose of the array *Pages* functions is to create a specific application page and display it in the working area. For example, the code for *OpenRecorderPage* is the following:

```
void OpenRecorderPage()
{
        // get next page ready
        RecorderPage* new_page = new RecorderPage();
```

Code for OpenRecorderPage *Continued*

```
        // create new page
        CurrentScreen->NewWorkArea(new_page);
        CurrentScreen->DisplayWorkArea();
    }
```

The first statement creates an object of class *RecorderPage*. This causes no changes on the screen, because the operation involves only the dynamic allocation of objects in memory. You can still see the page previously displayed in the working area. The next statement assigns the new page to the working area. Again, this operation has no effect on the screen. Note that before calling *OpenRecorderPage*, the class *PageSelector* deletes the page that occupied the working area. This operation only affects the memory dynamically allocated to the page, and this page still remains on the screen when OpenRecorderPage is called.

The last statement of *OpenRecorderPage* actually paints the new page inside the working area, covering the previously displayed page.

The array *Pages* is the bridge between the GUI and the application program. It is stored in the file *database.cpp* to emphasize its dependence on the application, and because it is a global variable. All the variables listed in database.cpp are global.

Listings 7.1 and 7.2 show the header and source code files for the *PageSelector* class. The *PageSelector* class is mainly a container class for the page buttons. In C++, containers are used to organize groups of interrelated objects of the same class.

Listing 7.1. The header file for class PageSelector.

```
#ifndef PAGESELECTORHPP
#define PAGESELECTORHPP

#include <string.h>

#include "database.hpp"
#include "box.hpp"
#include "graphics.hpp"
#include "legend.hpp"

#define PAGE_BUTTON_WIDTH 70

class PageSelector: public Icon {

    friend class PageButton;
    int button_selected;
    int total_buttons;
    PageButton* button [MAX_PAGE_BUTTON];
```

```
public:

    PageSelector();
    void Display();
    void Select(int);
    virtual ~PageSelector();
};


class PageButton: public Icon {

    friend class PageSelector;
    PageSelector* parent;
    void (*activation_function)();
    int page_number;
    Box* box;
    char descriptor [30];

    COLOR_TYPE border_color;
    COLOR_TYPE inactive_color;
    COLOR_TYPE active_color;
    COLOR_TYPE descriptor_color;

public:

    PageButton(PageSelector*, int, int, int,
            PAGE_BUTTON_DEFINITION*, int);
    void Display();
    void Highlight();
    void UnHighlight();
    void LeftButtonPressed();
    void LeftButtonReleased();
    virtual ~PageButton();
};

#endif
```

Listing 7.2. The implementation of class PageSelector.

```
#include "pagesel.hpp"
#include "screen.hpp"

PageSelector::PageSelector() : Icon(-1, -1, -1, -1)
{
    // assume all buttons are used, although the
    // actual number should be determined at this
    // time
    total_buttons = MAX_PAGE_BUTTON;
    button_selected = 0;
```

Listing 7.2 Continues

137

Listing 7.2 Continued

```
      // stop if no buttons to be created
      if (total_buttons == 0) return;

      // compute the height of each button
      int height = SCREEN_Y2 / total_buttons;

      // create all the buttons required
      for (int i = 0; i < total_buttons; i++) {
        int x = PAGE_SELECTOR_X1;
        int y = SCREEN_Y1 + height * i;
        button [i] = new PageButton(this, x, y, height,
                          &Pages [i], i);
      }
}

void PageSelector::Display()
{
      // display all the page selector buttons
      for (int i = 0; i < total_buttons; i++)
          button [i]->Display();
}

void PageSelector::Select(int page)
{
      // highlight the button for the new page
      button [button_selected]->UnHighlight();
      button_selected = page;
      button [button_selected]->Highlight();

      // load activation function
      void (*activation_function)() =
          button [button_selected]->activation_function;

      // eliminate the old page displayed
      CurrentScreen->ClearWorkArea();

      // invoke the button's activation function
      if (activation_function)
        (*activation_function)();
}


PageSelector::~PageSelector()
{
      // eliminate all the buttons
      for (int i = 0; i < total_buttons; i++)
        delete button [i];
}
```

```
PageButton::PageButton(PageSelector* parent_array,
                int x, int y, int size,
                PAGE_BUTTON_DEFINITION* pbp,
                int page) :
     Icon(x, y, x + PAGE_BUTTON_WIDTH, y + size)

{

     parent = parent_array;
     page_number = page;
     strncpy(descriptor,
          pbp->descriptor,
          sizeof(descriptor) );
     activation_function = pbp->activation_function;
     border_color = RED;
     inactive_color = CYAN;
     active_color = BRIGHT_CYAN;
     descriptor_color = BLACK;

     box = new Box(x1, y1, x2 - x1, y2 - y1,
                border_color, inactive_color);
}


void PageButton::Display()
{
     box->Display();

     BOX_TYPE title_box;
     title_box.x1 = x1;
     title_box.y1 = y1;
     title_box.x2 = x2;
     title_box.y2 = y2;
     Legend t_legend;
     t_legend.Center(&title_box,
                descriptor_color,
                descriptor);
}

void PageButton::LeftButtonPressed()
{
     Highlight();
}

void PageButton::LeftButtonReleased()
{
     parent->Select(page_number);
}

void PageButton::Highlight()
{
```

Listing 7.2 Continues

Listing 7.2 Continued

```
        box->Color(active_color);
        Display();
}

void PageButton::UnHighlight()
{
        box->Color(inactive_color);
        Display();
}

PageButton::~PageButton()
{
        delete box;
}
```

Function Descriptions

PageSelector::PageSelector

This class constructor creates the required page selector buttons. The necessary initialization information should be contained in the global array *Pages*, kept in the file *database.cpp*. As usual, the constructor doesn't modify the screen. Note that the screen coordinates passed to the base class constructor are off-screen. This procedure prevents an object of class *PageSelector* from responding to mouse clicks, because only its child buttons have this ability.

PageSelector::Display

All the buttons previously created are displayed. No button is initially selected, and they are all shown unhighlighted.

PageSelector::Select

Clicking one of the buttons causes this function to be invoked. The button previously highlighted returns to the inactive state, and the one selected is highlighted. The activation function you use is the one defined for the selected button in the array *Pages* in *database.cpp*. This function creates and displays a new page. It belongs to the GUI system, not the application.

PageSelector::~PageSelector

This function simply eliminates the objects allocated dynamically. The base class destructor cleans up the display list.

PageButton::PageButton

The class constructor links the object into the display list via the base class *Icon*, saves the relevant attributes passed, and creates a rectangular box in which to display the button. The screen is not modified.

PageButton::Display

This function paints a box and displays the button's legend centered inside the box.

PageButton::LeftButtonPressed

The screen handler invokes this function when you click the left mouse button. It provides visual feedback to the operator by highlighting the button. Note that the button previously selected on the page selector remains highlighted. Only when you release the button is a selection made.

PageButton::LeftButtonReleased

This function invokes the parent container class *PageSelector* to handle the deselecting of the previous selection and the selecting of the current button.

PageButton::Highlight

The button's repainting in a bright color indicates it is active.

PageButton::UnHighlight

This function restores the color of a button to its inactive state.

PageButton::~PageButton

The function relinquishes the dynamically allocated box and then allows the base class destructor to clean up the display list.

8

The Animation Class

Users of such common GUIs as Microsoft Windows will recognize the types of objects described so far. Once displayed, they all remain unchanged and stationary on the screen. Sometimes icons need to be different: they need the ability to modify themselves without explicit instructions from the user. These are animated icons.

You use animated objects all the time. Clocks run by themselves. Barometers, thermometers, speedometers, and fuel gauges all have behaviors the operator doesn't control directly (or even indirectly). A more complete example is a motion picture displayed in computer form or some type of animated simulation.

Some people regard animation as outside the domain of interfaces altogether. I believe that the basic machinery for animation belongs inside the GUI. Simple techniques make object animation feasible. This chapter shows how easy it is to support common animation demands.

The general structure of a GUI should not be upset by adding animation support. The extra machinery for animation should be transparent for objects that don't require it, and no overhead should be imposed on objects that are not animated.

The root class *Icon* is the starting point for animation. If the main program requests all objects in the display list to update their current displays, based on parameters internal to each object, the specific objects must animate themselves. Using a null virtual function called *Update* in class *Icon* ensures that objects incapable of animation do nothing.

To simplify the animation mechanism, the screen handler invokes each object in the display list after a single invocation of the *Update* function in class *Screen*. This action reduces the overhead in the top-level module to one line. The implementation is clean but not perfect. The loop time determines implicitly the update rate for the animated objects. Often you want the animation to proceed at a rigorous, time-scheduled rate. Such a rate entails a timer interrupt service routine in the event handler, which would invoke the screen's update function transparently from the top level (or event loop).

As a compromise, you could put some code in an icon's *Update* function that reads the system time and behaves accordingly. The digital clock described at the end of this chapter uses this approach. It's a simple solution, but it's not for general use, because it is inefficient to make each object read the time repeatedly

On the other hand, in many applications the value of some variable affects the appearance of an object. The application program itself manages the variable. Updates of this *control* variable are often random or completely asynchronous toward the GUI. Any value changes update the screen, so strict timing in the event loop is not critical.

Example 1: Designing a Ping-pong Ball

Here's a simple example to start the description of animated objects. In early video games, a popular game used a Ping-pong ball that bounced off the edges of a television screen. Using a vertical paddle, the player had to hit it to keep it out of a goal zone.

The class *PingPong* implements a ball that bounces around the screen by itself. There are no paddles to deal with, and the class doesn't really interact with the user. For run-time efficiency, a square ball is used instead of a round one because a square object is faster to draw and results in smoother animation. As an added feature, the program changes the color of the screen where the ball passes, eventually painting the entire screen in black. The demo disk has a page called PingPong, which shows three ping-pong balls in action.

The first thing needed to support motion is an animation function, which is called *Update()* in this book. This function needs to be called periodically so that objects can repaint themselves at a sufficient rate to give the impression of smooth motion. Listing 8.1 shows the header file for class *PingPong*.

Listing 8.1. The header file for class Ping-pong.

```
#ifndef PING-PONGHPP
#define PING-PONGHPP

#include "screen.hpp"
#include "graphics.hpp"

#define PING-PONG_WIDTH 10
#define PING-PONG_HEIGHT 6

class Ping-pong: public Icon {

    int x_direction;
    int y_direction;
    void Paint(COLOR_TYPE);
    void Erase();

public:

    Ping-pong(int, int);
    void Display();
    void Update();
};

#endif
```

The private variables `x_direction` and `y_direction` control the direction of travel. Positive x moves to the right, and positive y moves upward. The private function *Paint* displays the object in any given color. *Erase* makes the object disappear, and *Update* uses it to erase the object from its old position before showing it at its new one. Listing 8.2. shows the full implementation of the class.

Listing 8.2. The implementation of class Ping-pong.

```
#include "ping-pong.hpp"

Ping-pong::Ping-pong(int x, int y) :
    Icon(x, y, x + PING-PONG_WIDTH, y + PING-
PONG_HEIGHT)
{
```

Listing 8.2 Continues

145

Listing 8.2 Continued

```
      /* start the object moving toward upper right */
      x_direction = 1;
      y_direction = 1;
}

void Ping-pong::Display()
{
      Paint(WHITE);
}

void Ping-pong::Erase()
{
      Paint(BLACK);
}

void Ping-pong::Paint(COLOR_TYPE color)
{
      BOX_TYPE box;
      box.x1 = x1;
      box.y1 = y1;
      box.x2 = x1 + PING-PONG_WIDTH;
      box.y2 = y1 + PING-PONG_HEIGHT;
      GraphicsHandler->DrawBox(color, SOLID_LINE, &box);
}

void Ping-pong::Update()
{
      int x, y;

      // erase the old box;
      Erase();

      // move the box
      x1 += x_direction;
      if ( (x1 < 1) || (x1 + PING-PONG_WIDTH > WORK_PAGE_X2) )
        x_direction = -x_direction;

      y1 += y_direction;
      if ( (y1 < 1) ||
          (y1 + PING-PONG_HEIGHT > SCREEN_TITLE_Y1 - 2)
)
        y_direction = -y_direction;

      // show the new location
      Display();
}
```

The class is surprisingly short, unlike listings that go on for countless pages. The program also works! You can create an army of additional Ping-pong balls in class *Ping-pongPage* (in the file *ball.cpp*). They bounce around the screen at the same time, each following its own trajectory, unaware of the existence of the others. The speed of each object does decrease as you add more objects because of the processing time required to update the screen for each object.

The class has no destructor. The base class has all the code needed to do the job, because *Ping-pong* contains no dynamically allocated objects created inside. The following sections contain a brief explanation of each function.

Function Descriptions

Ping-pong::Ping-pong

The class constructor registers the object's screen coordinates through the base class, which also attaches it to the display list. The initialized direction of travel is to the right and upward. No changes are made to the screen.

Ping-pong::Display

This function paints a small rectangular box on the screen. The border is white, and the inside is the background color of the work area.

Ping-pong::Erase

This function erases the Ping-pong object from the screen for repainting at a different location. It is a private function. Displaying the object's outline in black performs the erasing operation.

Ping-pong::Paint

This function paints the object in any screen color. It is a private function used by *Display* and *Erase*.

Ping-pong::Update

This is the actual animation support function. The screen handler function *Screen::Update* invokes it, along with every object in the display list. Class *Ping-pong* only modifies its screen coordinates by one pixel in the direction of motion. If the Ping-pong balls hit a screen edge, the direction of motion reverses. Before displaying itself at the new location, the old image is painted in black. The object leaves a permanent black wake as it moves. This form of graphic animation is the simplest as well as the slowest.

In the next example, nothing changes except the part being repainted. When dealing with something like a cartoon in a video game, you can create memory-resident objects representing successive instances of each object. Using a BitBlt pixel copy function between memory and screen would be faster than completely repainting the object.

Example 2: Designing an Animated Water Tank

This example deals with objects that are stationary on-screen. Only part of the object changes, without disturbing the objects position. The object is a *vat*, simply a tank used in industry to mix liquids. Assume that the vat is connected to input and output pipes, although for simplicity the pipes are not shown here. A more sophisticated system could also show pumps or valves used to fill and empty the vat. The tank looks like the one in figure 8.1.

Fig. 8.1. A vat used to store water.

Part of the object is invariant, including the box enclosing the tank, the box around the tank's title, and the title itself. The variant part is the level of the fluid stored inside. This is the part handled by the animation function. Before writing any code, you need to decide how to subdivide the implementation of the vat — in other words, how many subclasses to use. This example uses one box for the title area and one for the rest of the object. The animated part uses graphics functions, but no dynamically allocated objects are created or handled. A more sophisticated object could use a different approach.

A function is needed to paint a filled-in area that represents fluid, and a control variable must be used to indicate how much fluid there is. It could be a floating point value between 0 and 1, with the latter indicating a full tank. For efficiency, the function should paint only changes in fluid level, not all the fluid in the tank. Painting the entire fluid contents every time the function is executed is a waste of processing time. To paint changes, there needs to be a function that adds fluid by extending the fluid area, and one that removes fluid by erasing part of the fluid area.

The animation machinery should drive both these painting functions, and they are best left as private member functions. The implementation is straightforward. Listing 8.3 shows the header file for class *Vat*. The demo program on the companion disk has a page called *Tanks*, shown in figure 8.2.

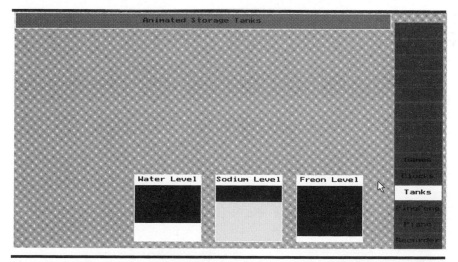

Fig. 8.2. The layout of page Tanks.

Listing 8.3. The header file for class Vat.

```
#ifndef VATHPP
#define VATHPP

#include <string.h>

#include "icon.hpp"
#include "box.hpp"
#include "graphics.hpp"
#include "legend.hpp"

#define VAT_WIDTH 100
#define VAT_HEIGHT 100
#define VAT_LEGEND_HEIGHT 15


class Vat: public Icon {

        int fluid_x1, fluid_y1, fluid_x2, fluid_y2;
        Box* fluid_level;
        Box* title_box;

        char vat_legend [20];
        float* current_level;
        float flow_increment;
        int fluid_height;

        COLOR_TYPE border_color;
        COLOR_TYPE fill_color;
        COLOR_TYPE fluid_color;

        void DecreaseLevel(int);
        void IncreaseLevel(int);
        int Level(float);

public:

        Vat(int, int, char*, float*, COLOR_TYPE);
        void Display();
        void Update();
        ~Vat();
};

#endif
```

Listing 8.4. The implementation of class Vat.

```
#include "vat.hpp"

Vat::Vat(int x, int y, char* string, float*
initial_value,
COLOR_TYPE color) :
```

```
        Icon(x, y, x + VAT_WIDTH, y + VAT_HEIGHT)
{
    current_level = initial_value;
    strcpy(vat_legend, string);
    fluid_x1= x;
    fluid_y1 = y + 1;
    fluid_x2 = x + VAT_WIDTH;
    fluid_y2 = y + VAT_HEIGHT - VAT_LEGEND_HEIGHT;

    fluid_height = 0;
    flow_increment = 0.01;

    border_color = YELLOW;
    fill_color = BLACK;
    fluid_color = color;

    fluid_level = new Box(x1, y1,
            x2 - x1,
            VAT_HEIGHT - VAT_LEGEND_HEIGHT,
            border_color,
            fill_color);

    title_box = new Box(x1, y2 - VAT_LEGEND_HEIGHT,
            x2 - x1,
            VAT_LEGEND_HEIGHT,
            border_color,
            border_color);
}

void Vat::Display()
{
    fluid_level->Display();
    title_box->Display();

    // partition off the legend area
    BOX_TYPE title;
    title.x1 = x1;
    title.y1 = y2 - VAT_LEGEND_HEIGHT;
    title.x2 = x2;
    title.y2 = y2;
    Legend title_legend;
    title_legend.Center(&title, BLACK, vat_legend);

    // assume no part of the fluid is currently shown,
    // so the fluid level gets updated
    fluid_height = 0;
        Update();
    }
```

Listing 8.4 Continues

Listing 8.4 Continued

```
void Vat::Update()
{
      *current_level += flow_increment;

      if (*current_level >= 0.99)
        flow_increment = -0.01;

      if (*current_level <= 0.01)
        flow_increment = 0.01;

      int level = Level(*current_level);

      if (level > fluid_height)
        IncreaseLevel(level);
      else
        DecreaseLevel(level);
}

void Vat::DecreaseLevel(int level)
{
      // erase excess part of fluid
      BOX_TYPE box;
      box.x1 = fluid_x1 + 1;
      box.y1 = fluid_y1 + level;
      box.x2 = fluid_x2 - 2;
      box.y2 = fluid_y1 + fluid_height;
      GraphicsHandler->FillBox(fill_color, &box);

      // adjust vat fluid coordinate
      fluid_height = level;
}

void Vat::IncreaseLevel(int level)
{
      // add a piece to the fluid
      BOX_TYPE box;
      box.x1 = fluid_x1 + 1;
      box.y1 = fluid_y1 + fluid_height;
      box.x2 = fluid_x2 - 2;
      box.y2 = fluid_y1 + level;
      GraphicsHandler->FillBox(fluid_color, &box);

      // adjust vat fluid coordinate
      fluid_height = level;
}

int Vat::Level(float value)
{
      // convert the setting from range (0..1) to the proper
      // range
```

```
        return value * (fluid_y2 - 1 - fluid_y1);
}

Vat::~Vat()
{
    delete fluid_level;
    delete title_box;
}
```

Function Descriptions

Vat::Vat

The class constructor receives a pointer to the object's control variable. In a real-world situation, the application program would set this variable, possibly through an interrupt handler monitoring a remote fluid-level sensor. By changing this variable, the interface program would update the screen to keep it current.

Copying the object's title into a character array guarantees correct operation of class *Vat*, even if the function invoking the class constructor no longer stores the title itself. The constructor stores the colors used by the object and then sets up the two dynamically allocated boxes. As usual, the display itself is not updated.

Vat::Display

This function displays the box around the overall tank and the one around the title, centering the title string inside its own box. To force the *Update* function to paint the complete water contents, the function sets the `fluid_height` variable to zero. To see how, examine the code for the *Update* function. The screen is modified only by sensing a change in fluid level. Setting the value of **fluid_height** to zero guarantees sensing a change in level the first time *Update* is called.

Vat::Update

This function changes the fluid level displayed. It increases the level in 1% increments until the tank is completely full and then empties it in 1% steps, repeating the process indefinitely.

Vat::DecreaseLevel

This private function is called when the tank's fluid level drops. Erasing the excess fluid lowers the level. Because changes in level are often small between successive updates, the area erased is small, and the function works quickly.

Vat::IncreaseLevel

When Vat::Update determines that the level in the vat has risen, it calls the private function IncreaseLevel. This function is fast because it paints only the additional fluid, not the entire fluid contents.

Vat::Level

This private function gets the value of the fluid level control variable (whose range is 0..1) and computes the corresponding height of the fluid to display.

Vat::~Vat

The class destructor relinquishes the two boxes' memory used by the tank. The base class *Icon* cleans up the display list.

Example 3: Designing a Digital Clock

The last example illustrates the implementation of a digital clock. A clock is merely a digital readout device whose control variable is the computer's system time. In generic digital readouts, the application program controls the variable, which represents the value of some physical entity such as body temperature, video luminance, atmospheric humidity, and so on. Any change in the control variable automatically entails an update of the value shown on the digital readout.

There are many ways of implementing computer clocks. Besides deciding whether to use a digital or analog format, the design must involve the clock's interaction with other objects on the screen.

In this example, the clock is digital. Any application program can create one on the screen. Its integration into the display list is seamless. After creation a clock is autonomous: you don't have to deal with its details. Moreover, you can create a clock showing the time in any arbitrary world time zone, and you can have multiple clocks on the screen simultaneously.

To maintain independence from specific C++ implementations and operating systems, the class uses the function *CurrentTime* from class *Events* to read the time. Displaying the current time is straightforward: the operating system provides the system time, which is then converted to string format and centered inside a rectangular box.

Handling time zones is more difficult. World time zones *usually* differ from Greenwich Mean Time (GMT) by an integer number of hours, but not always. For example, India is 5:30 hours ahead of GMT, Newfoundland is behind by 3:30 hours, and Chatham Island, east of New Zealand, is 12:45 hours ahead.

A floating-point value is used to indicate the offset of a clock's time from some reference time. GMT could be used as a reference, but because a user is usually concerned about the local time, I'll use that time as the reference. Each clock must also carry a description field that indicates the city or country it relates to. Using a 24-hour format avoids the nonstandard A.M. and P.M. designators. Figure 8.3 shows the layout required.

Fig. 8.3. The layout for the digital clock.

The demo program has a page called *Clocks* with three independent clocks running on different time zones. Figure 8.4 shows the page.

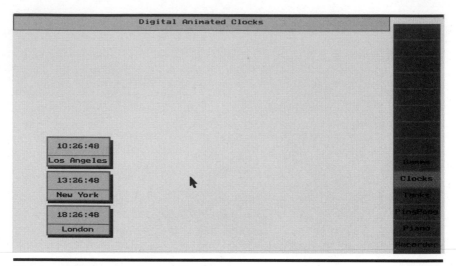

Fig. 8.4. The layout of page Clocks.

The following listings show the header and source files for class *Clock*.

Listing 8.5. The header file for class Clock.

```
#ifndef CLOCKHPP
#define CLOCKHPP

#include "icon.hpp"
#include "box.hpp"
#include "graphics.hpp"
#include "events.hpp"

#define CLOCK_WIDTH 95
#define CLOCK_HEIGHT 44
#define CLOCK_LEGEND_HEIGHT 14

class Clock: public Icon {

protected:

    char time_zone [20];
    ShadedBox* box;
    float time_difference;
    long current_time;

public:

    Clock(int, int, char* = "", float = 0);
    virtual void Display();
```

```
        virtual void Update();
        virtual ~Clock();
};

#endif
```

Listing 8.6. The implementation of class Clock.

```
#include "clock.hpp"
#include "time.h"
#include "legend.hpp"
#include <string.h>

Clock::Clock(int x, int y, char* title, float
offset) :
    Icon(x, y, x + CLOCK_WIDTH, y + CLOCK_HEIGHT)
{
    // make a copy of the button's name
    if (strlen(title) == 0) {
      title = "Local Time";
      time_difference = 0;
    }
    // use the requested time zone and difference
    strncpy(time_zone, title, sizeof(time_zone) );
    time_difference = offset;

    // initialize the time
    current_time = 0;

    // create the clock box
    box = new ShadedBox(x1, y1,
                  x2 - x1, y2 - y1,
                  BLACK,
                  BRIGHT_RED,
                  GRAY);
}

void Clock::Display()
{
    // show the backdrop box
    box->Display();

    // partition off the legend area
    BOX_TYPE area;
    area.x1 = x1 + 2;
    area.y1 = y1 + CLOCK_LEGEND_HEIGHT + 2;
    area.x2 = x2 - 2;
    area.y2 = area.y1;
    GraphicsHandler->DrawLine(BRIGHT_RED,
                    SOLID_LINE,
```

Listing 8.6 Continues

Listing 8.6 Continued

```
                                &area);

        // display the name of the time zone
        Legend time;
        area.y1 = y1;
        time.Center(&area, BRIGHT_RED, time_zone);
    }

    void Clock::Update()
    {
        // display the complete clock if not running
        if (current_time == 0) Display();

        // see if the time has changed
        long new_time = EventsHandler->SystemTime();
        if (new_time == current_time) return;

        // update the time
        current_time = new_time;

        // read the time for our time zone
        char* our_time =
                EventsHandler-
>CurrentTime(time_difference);

        // don't let mouse interrupts disrupt the
        // process of updating the screen
        EventsHandler->DisableInterrupts();

        // erase the old time
        BOX_TYPE box;
        box.x1 = x1 + 3;
        box.y1 = y1 + CLOCK_LEGEND_HEIGHT + 3;
        box.x2 = x2 - 3;
        box.y2 = y2 - 3;
        GraphicsHandler->FillBox(GRAY, &box);

        // display the current time
        Legend time;
        time.Center(&box, BRIGHT_RED, our_time);

        // display updates: turn on the interrupts
        EventsHandler->EnableInterrupts();
    }

    Clock::~Clock()

        delete box;
    }
```

The local variables in class *Clock* are declared `protected` in order to allow classes derived from *Clock* to access them directly.

Function Descriptions

Clock::Clock

The class constructor uses default values for the parameters ***title*** and ***offset***. Creating the clock for the local time zone is simplified by using these defaults, which result in the string "Local Time" displayed on the clock. If a string is passed to the constructor, the string is used as the clock's time zone instead of the default string. The variable ***current_time*** is set to zero to force the animation function *Update()* to start the clock running. The constructor does not modify the screen.

Clock::Display

This function paints a shaded box to enclose the clock and then closes off a bottom area where the time-zone legend centers. No time shows up, because this action is reserved for the *Update* function.

Clock::Update

This function checks whether the clock has already started. If not, it paints the entire object. Then the system time is read in the format hour:minutes:seconds. The time is given in 24-hour format. If the new time is different from the time displayed, it is displayed and it erases the old time. A possible improvement: determining which fields of the clock's time have changed and erasing and repainting only those fields.

Clock::~Clock

The destructor relinquishes the dynamically allocated box object created in the constructor and then lets the base class destructor clean up the display list. The screen is not modified.

9

The Popup Class

The screen objects described so far have one thing in common: once a specific page is selected, all its individual controls are displayed. To show other controls, a different page must be selected. Objects of class *Popup* don't behave this way. They are activated when special buttons are pressed, and they display themselves directly on top of anything already on the page. They are like a window opened in the middle of the page showing objects behind it. Closing the window causes the window to disappear, making any covered objects reappear.

Most popular computer programs have objects that pop up on the screen. Borland International's best-seller SideKick is one program with many popup objects. The dialog boxes used in Microsoft Windows are another example.

Pop-up windows in this book are compound objects made up by a box that encloses a number of control icons which are somehow related. These pop-up objects are different from, say, Borland SideKick pop-up menus because they can appear only on certain GUI pages. Also, rather than being triggered by hot keys, they are created by clicking a special icon called a *PopupWindowButton*. The idea behind the use of a pop-up object is to reduce the number of controls displayed on a page. Many times, a page contains control icons that are used only infrequently. These icons should be accessible on a given page, but they shouldn't always be fully displayed, to avoid cluttering the screen. Consider for example a configuration menu. If a small button on the screen were labeled *Configuration*, it could represent the entire menu. Pressing this button could open a pop-up panel of configuration controls. This panel would partially cover a portion of the work area. When the configuration operations were complete, the panel could be closed, restoring the screen to its previous state.

Such a use of pop-up windows allows a GUI to display less data at a given time, making for an interface that is easier to understand. A pop-up icon can be viewed as a parenthesis in the normal page activity, enclosing a set of operations used only rarely.

Popup windows usually show controls, not text, in this context. Error messages and alarm conditions normally use the popup paradigm, but normal text input/output might use a different approach. Popup objects can add information to a page, but only when necessary. They also show this information without losing the page context itself. You could relegate most information shown on a page to a series of popup windows. Should you use pages or popup windows? To keep a simple user model of the system, you should use the clean separation provided by pages to distinguish an application's various tasks. At the end of this chapter is a simple program that uses a popup window.

Efficiency Considerations

Windows that pop up in the middle of a page must be implemented in a manner that allows the screen to be restored when the window is closed. There are basically two approaches for doing this: the first one data-intensive and the second code-intensive. Many commercial windowing packages use the first method. When a window is opened, the area covered is copied pixel-by-pixel to a buffer allocated dynamically on the heap. The operation of moving a pixel bit map from one area of memory to another is known as a *BitBlt* (pronounced *bit-blit*), which indicates a block transfer of binary data. To restore the background image after closing the window, the BitBlt is performed in the opposite direction, and the memory buffer is returned to the heap. This approach is very straightforward, but it has two serious—sometimes unsolvable—drawbacks.

The first problem is the time required for these memory allocations and block transfers. When objects must appear on the screen, an operator tolerates only minimal delays. Much screen activity, as in a complex dynamic system, creates substantial overhead in pixel processing, especially when large screen areas are involved.

The second problem is the risk of running out of memory without warning. How much heap memory is necessary? A screen with 640 x 350 four-bit pixels, the least needed for graphics, uses more than 100K of RAM. Covering one-fourth of the screen requires a 25K memory block to save the underlying image. Several popup objects involved at once can easily outstrip the memory available.

The designer cannot always know beforehand the number and size of objects used at run-time. Moreover, most personal computers have little heap memory. The amount is a few hundred kilobytes at most in MS-DOS, so memory-allocation failures quickly show up at run-time.

The code-intensive approach uses no BitBlt operations or heap allocations. The nature of the display list makes it easy to determine which objects need to be repainted, and the objects can then be called on to repaint themselves. The abstract class *Popup* handles screen restoration through its destructor, by requesting the screen handler to repaint any object that utilized pixels inside a given region of the screen. Because all this is performed through a destructor, no explicit function calls are required by windows derived from class *Popup*, and the screen-restoration process is completely transparent.

Implementation

The popup windows in this chapter share a common set of display features. They are all displayed as a box with shading on the right and the bottom sides. Their positions and dimensions can be set as desired, but for the sake of simplicity, the color attributes are fixed. Figure 9.1 shows the layout of a popup window.

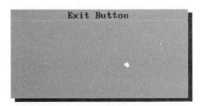

Fig. 9.1. The general layout for a popup window.

The top area, a button, closes the popup window. The legend is also the title of the window itself. The window box inserted in the screen list has no behavior if clicked. Only its exit button and child controls are active.

Popup buttons and popup windows have a one-to-one relationship. Only a popup button can create a popup window. Clicking or touching a popup button opens its associated window. The window, if open, is destroyed when the button is. Each button can open only one window. Multiple clicking of the button opens only one window.

Think of a popup button as the parent of a popup window. In a parent-child relationship, the child's actions must go also to the parent, for multiple child icons can be organized under a single parent. Look what happens when you click the exit button. It does nothing but delete its parent window. The parent window then closes the window and sends a signal to its parent. This message activity is a delicate process, but it adds a tremendous amount of power. The following figure shows the salient actions involved in clicking the exit button of a popup window. Listings 9.1 and 9.2 show the header file for the *Popup* class.

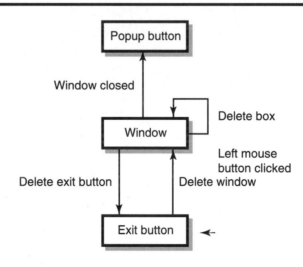

Fig. 9.2. The managing activity resulting from a mouse click on a popup window's exit button.

Listing 9.1. The header file for class Popup.

```
#ifndef POPUPHPP
#define POPUPHPP

#include <string.h>

#include "box.hpp"
#include "screen.hpp"
#include "graphics.hpp"
#include "limit.hpp"
#include "legend.hpp"
#include "database.hpp"

#define POPUP_BUTTON_WIDTH 70
#define POPUP_BUTTON_HEIGHT 38

class PopupWindowButton : public Icon {

    friend class PopupWindow;
    friend class PopupWindowExitButton;

    ShadedBox* box;
    PopupWindow* window;
    void (*open_window)(PopupWindowButton*);
    char *text1;
    char *text2;
    COLOR_TYPE text_color;
    COLOR_TYPE shade_color;
    COLOR_TYPE border_color;
    COLOR_TYPE fill_color;
    COLOR_TYPE inactive_color;
    COLOR_TYPE active_color;

public:

    PopupWindowButton(void (PopupWindowButton*),
            int, int, int, int, char*, char*);
    void Display();
    int WindowOpened() { return window ? 1 : 0; }
    void Highlight();
    void UnHighlight();
    void LeftButtonPressed();
    void LeftButtonReleased();
    virtual ~PopupWindowButton();
};


#define POPUP_WINDOW_LEGEND_HEIGHT 20

class PopupWindow : public Icon {
```

Listing 9.1 Continues

Listing 9.1 Continued

```
        friend class PopupWindowButton;
        friend class PopupWindowExitButton;

        ShadedBox* box;
        PopupWindowButton* parent_button;
        PopupWindowExitButton* exit_button;

        COLOR_TYPE shade_color;
        COLOR_TYPE border_color;
        COLOR_TYPE inactive_color;
        COLOR_TYPE active_color;
        COLOR_TYPE title_color;
        COLOR_TYPE title_backdrop_color;

public:

        PopupWindow(PopupWindowButton*, int, int,
                int, int, char*);
        virtual void Display();
        virtual ~PopupWindow();
};


class PopupWindowExitButton: public Icon {

        friend class TitleBox;
        PopupWindow* parent_window;
        TopShadedBox* top_box;
        char legend [MAX_LEGEND_LENGTH + 1];

        COLOR_TYPE inactive_color;
        COLOR_TYPE active_color;
        COLOR_TYPE legend_color;
        COLOR_TYPE shade_color;
        COLOR_TYPE border_color;
        COLOR_TYPE fill_color;

public:

        PopupWindowExitButton(PopupWindow*, char*,
                COLOR_TYPE,
                COLOR_TYPE,
                COLOR_TYPE,
                COLOR_TYPE,
                COLOR_TYPE,
                int, int, int, int);
        void Display();
        void LeftButtonPressed();
        void LeftButtonReleased();
        virtual ~PopupWindowExitButton();
};

        #endif
```

Listing 9.2. The implementation of class Popup.

```cpp
#include "popup.hpp"

PopupWindowButton::PopupWindowButton(
                void (*open)(PopupWindowButton*),
                int x1, int y1, int x2, int y2,
                char *mtext1, char *mtext2) :
                Icon(x1, y1, x2, y2)
{
    open_window = open;
    window = 0;
    text1 = mtext1;
    text2 = mtext2;

    text_color =  BRIGHT_CYAN;
    shade_color = BLACK;
    border_color = YELLOW;
    inactive_color = BRIGHT_BLUE;
    active_color =  YELLOW;
    fill_color = inactive_color;
    box = new ShadedBox(x1, y1, x2 - x1, y2 - y1,
                        shade_color,
                        border_color,
                        fill_color);
}

void PopupWindowButton::Display()
{
    box->Display();

    BOX_TYPE title_box;
    title_box.x1 = x1;
    title_box.y1 = y1;
    title_box.x2 = x2;
    title_box.y2 = y2;
    Legend title_legend;
    title_legend.Center(&title_box, text_color,
                text1, text2);
}


void PopupWindowButton::LeftButtonPressed()
{
    box->Color(active_color);
    Display();
}

void PopupWindowButton::LeftButtonReleased()
{
```

Listing 9.2 Continues

Listing 9.2 Continued

```
      box->Color(inactive_color);
      Display();

      // exit if a window is already open
      if (window) return;

      if (open_window)
        (*open_window)(this);
}


PopupWindowButton::~PopupWindowButton()
{
      delete box;

      // remove the button before the window
      // it might have opened
      CurrentScreen->RemoveItem(this);

      if (window)
        delete window;
}


PopupWindow::PopupWindow(PopupWindowButton* parent,
              int x1, int y1, int x2, int y2,
              char* ptitle) :
              Icon(x1, y1, x2, y2)
{
      parent_button = parent;
      parent_button->window = this;

      title_color =  BRIGHT_CYAN;
      title_backdrop_color =  BRIGHT_CYAN;
      shade_color = BLACK;
      border_color = YELLOW;
      inactive_color = GRAY;
      active_color = WHITE;

      box = new ShadedBox(x1, y1, x2 - x1, y2 - y1,
                          shade_color,
                          border_color,
                          inactive_color);

      exit_button = new PopupWindowExitButton(this, ptitle,
          shade_color,
          border_color,
          inactive_color,
          active_color,
          title_color,
```

```
                x1,
                y2 - POPUP_WINDOW_LEGEND_HEIGHT,
                x2, y2);
}

void PopupWindow::Display()
{
      box->Display();
      exit_button->Display();
}


PopupWindow::~PopupWindow()
{
      delete box;
      delete exit_button;

      parent_button->window = 0;

      // remove item from screen list
      // before you repaint the screen.
      // include the shaded areas too.
      CurrentScreen->RemoveItem(this);
      CurrentScreen->ReDraw(x1, y1 - 3, x2 + 3, y2);
}

PopupWindowExitButton::PopupWindowExitButton(PopupWindow* parent,
                  char* title,
                  COLOR_TYPE shade_clr,
                  COLOR_TYPE border_clr,
                  COLOR_TYPE inactive_clr,
                  COLOR_TYPE active_clr,
                  COLOR_TYPE legend_clr,
                  int x1, int y1, int x2, int y2) :
                  Icon(x1, y1, x2, y2)

{
      parent_window = parent;
      strncpy(legend, title, sizeof(legend) );

      shade_color = shade_clr;
      border_color = border_clr;
      fill_color = inactive_color = inactive_clr;
      active_color = active_clr;
      legend_color = legend_clr;

      top_box = new TopShadedBox(x1, y1, x2-x1, y2-y1,
                        shade_color, border_color,
      fill_color);
      }
```

Listing 9.2 Continues

Listing 9.2 Continued

```
void PopupWindowExitButton::Display()
{
      top_box->Display();

      // add BOTTOM border lines
      BOX_TYPE bottom_border;
      bottom_border.x1 = x1 + 2;
      bottom_border.y1 = y1;
      bottom_border.x2 = x2 - 4;
      bottom_border.y2 = y1 + 1;
      GraphicsHandler->FillBox(border_color, &bottom_border);

      // display exit button title
      BOX_TYPE title_box;
      title_box.x1 = x1;
      title_box.y1 = y1;
      title_box.x2 = x2;
      title_box.y2 = y2;
      Legend title_legend;
      title_legend.Center(&title_box, legend_color, legend);
}


void PopupWindowExitButton::LeftButtonPressed()
{
      top_box->Color(active_color);
      Display();
}

void PopupWindowExitButton::LeftButtonReleased()
{
      delete parent_window;
}

PopupWindowExitButton::~PopupWindowExitButton()
{
      delete top_box;
}
```

Function Descriptions

PopupWindowButton::PopupWindowButton

This function registers the state variables for the button and creates the backdrop box needed. It displays nothing on the screen, but it saves a reference to the function responsible for opening the popup window.

PopupWindowButton::Display

This function displays the button as a shaded box with a legend centered inside.

PopupWindowButton::WindowOpened

This public-access function returns a Boolean variable indicating whether a popup button's window is open. It is used mainly on two occasions:

1. After you click a popup button, this function determines whether the popup window is already open, in order to avoid opening more than one.

2. After you delete a popup button, this function sees whether an associated popup window should also be deleted. An open window is deleted along with its parent button.

PopupWindowButton::Highlight

PopupWindowButton::UnHighlight

These functions, declared but not implemented, remain as an exercise for the reader. Class *PopupButton* uses these generic functions, employed by most other icons shown in this book, only once in the code described.

PopupWindowButton::LeftButtonPressed

This function makes the button change color when you click it. No other action takes place until you release the mouse button.

PopupWindowButton::LeftButtonReleased

This function restores the button to its original color and opens the popup window associated with it, if not already open. A pointer to the new popup window returns to the parent button. The parent uses this pointer to send messages to the child window.

PopupWindowButton::~PopupWindowButton

This function cleans up the display list (through the base class destructor), and it closes and deletes any open popup windows.

PopupWindow::PopupWindow

This constructor saves the state variables and the pointer to the parent button. It also creates the box and exit buttons used by all popup windows. Nothing is displayed.

PopupWindow::Display

This function paints an empty popup window on the screen, showing a box with an exit button at the top.

PopupWindow::~PopupWindow

This destructor cleans up the dynamically allocated icons and closes the window by repainting the objects covered by it.

PopupWindowExitButton::PopupWindowExitButton

This constructor registers a few state attributes and creates a button that appears at the top of the popup window. The parent of a *PopupWindowExitButton* is a *PopupWindow*. You must save a reference to the parent in the exit button object to notify the parent when the child is activated. No changes are made to the screen.

PopupWindowExitButton::Display

This function displays the exit button as a button occupying the top portion of a popup window. It has a legend centered on it, showing the name of the window.

PopupWindowExitButton::LeftButtonPressed

This function makes the exit button change color when you click the mouse on it. No action occurs until the mouse is released.

PopupWindowExitButton::LeftButtonReleased

This function deletes the parent window, which in turn will delete the window's box and the exit button. Any items covered will then reappear on the screen.

PopupWindowExitButton::~PopupWindowExitButton

This destructor relinquishes the memory allocated for the box and then uses the base-class destructor to clean up the display list.

A Quick Example

Now that you have seen what the basic objects look like and how they work, it's time to put them together into a simple application. Suppose you decide on a program to control a digital tape recorder via a SCSI interface or an IEEE-488 bus. You need to assemble the needed controls on the screen, probably grouping them onto a single page. Because you'll seldom use the controls for setting up the audio response, they are relegated to a special popup window. You can see a program like this in the demo program. It's on the companion disk, on the page *Recorder*. The page looks like the one shown in figure 9.3.

The button labled SETUP CONTROLS is a *PopupButton*. If ypu press it you get a popup window with additional controls on it. The screen then looks like the one shown in figure 9.4.

The popup window obscures the button that generated it. But the *PopupButton* knows whether you've opened its child window. To close the window, click in the window's title area. The files needed by class *SetupPopup* are shown in listing 9.3.

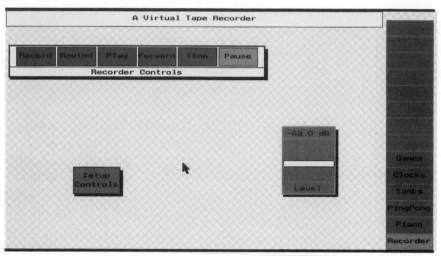

Fig. 9.3 The Recorder *page with the popup window closed.*

Listing 9.3. The header file for class SetupPop.

```
#ifndef SETUPHPP
#define SETUPHPP

#include "popup.hpp"
#include "pot.hpp"
#include "pushbut.hpp"
#include "selector.hpp"
#include "graphics.hpp"

#define SETUP_WINDOW_WIDTH 365
#define SETUP_WINDOW_HEIGHT 210
#define SETUP_WINDOW_LEGEND_HEIGHT 25

class SetupPopup: public PopupWindow {

        ToneLevelPot* bass;
        ToneLevelPot* treble;
        HorizontalSelector* source;
        BistablePushButton* defeat;

        COLOR_TYPE shade_color;
        COLOR_TYPE border_color;
        COLOR_TYPE fill_color;
        COLOR_TYPE title_color;
        COLOR_TYPE title_backdrop_color;

public:
```

```
      SetupPopup(PopupWindowButton*, int, int, char*);
      void Display();
      virtual ~SetupPopup();
};


void OpenSetupPopup(PopupWindowButton*);

#endif
```

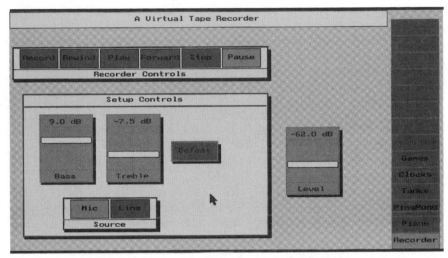

Fig. 9.4 The Recorder page with the popup window open.

Listing 9.4. The implementation of class SetupPopup.

```
#include "setup.hpp"
#include "database.hpp"

SetupPopup::SetupPopup(PopupWindowButton* parent,
        int x, int y, char* mtitle) :
        PopupWindow(parent, x, y,
         x + SETUP_WINDOW_WIDTH, y +
SETUP_WINDOW_HEIGHT,
        mtitle)
{
    title_color = BRIGHT_CYAN;
    title_backdrop_color =  BRIGHT_CYAN;
    shade_color = BLACK;
    border_color = YELLOW;
    fill_color = BRIGHT_BLUE;
```

Listing 9.4 Continues

Listing 9.4 Continued

```
        bass = new ToneLevelPot(x + 25, y + 80,
                "Bass",
                &RecorderSettings. bass,
                0);

        treble = new ToneLevelPot(x + 125, y + 80,
                "Treble",
                &RecorderSettings. treble,
                0);

        source = new HorizontalSelector(x + 60, y + 10,
                "Source",
                &RecorderSettings. source,
                0,
                "Mic", "Line");

        defeat = new BistablePushButton(x + 220, y + 110,
                "Defeat", &RecorderSettings. defeat,
                0);
}

void SetupPopup::Display()
{
        PopupWindow::Display();

        bass->Display();
        treble->Display();
        source->Display();
        defeat->Display();
}

SetupPopup::~SetupPopup()
{

        delete bass;
        delete treble;
        delete source;
        delete defeat;
}


void OpenSetupPopup(PopupWindowButton* parent)
{
        SetupPopup* window = new SetupPopup(parent, 20, 20,
                        "Setup Controls");
        window->Display();
}
```

Function Descriptions

SetupPopup::SetupPopup

The class constructor defines the colors used in the window, although you could standardize them for all popup windows. All the popup controls are created, but no changes are made to the screen.

SetupPopup::Display

This function invokes the base class to display the window framework and then paints the individual controls in the window.

SetupPopup::~SetupPopup

The destructor deletes the controls shown in the popup window; then the base class destructor is automatically invoked to delete and close the window.

OpenSetupPopup

This function is *not* part of class *SetupPopup*. It creates an instance of class *SetupPopup* and displays it on-screen, overlaying it in the work area. The popup button labeled SETUP in the demo program receives a pointer to this function. This function is the activation function for the SETUP button. Each popup button in a GUI has its own application-specific activation function. Clicking the popup button invokes its activation function for the processing needed to open the associated popup winow.

The Configuration Object

Today's complex programs require some configuration in order to meet the requirements of disparate users. You might want different levels in a program with menus, based upon the user's level of expertise. When using files, you might want to let the user establish certain default filenames permanently. Allowing the user to configure a program is the best way to tailor a single program to varying needs. Who knows these needs better than the user?

Do You Need One?

Consider a typical GUI control application, such as a computer-based digital storage oscilloscope (DSO). The system might have a data-acquisition card, or it might be connected to a DSO via an IEEE-488 bus. The control page has selectors, buttons, potentiometers, and popup icons. If you turn the system off and then back on again with all these adjustable controls, you need to find the settings as you left them. The same goes for any customizations you made to the program, such as object colors or positions. All this entails that you send certain commands to the remote devices (like the DSO) so the settings on the screen correspond to those selected by the hardware. Thus the GUI must execute some initialization code before it shows anything on the screen. Moreover, you must store some data on disk when you exit the program and then load it into the system when you run the application program again.

The Implementation

Obviously you can write a few C functions to perform the saving and restoring of variables and call them when starting and ending the program. A better way, more consistent with C++ methods, is to use an object whose scope is global. Such an object invokes its constructor automatically when created and its destructor when the object goes out of scope. Use global objects with great care in C++. There is no guarantee of their order of initialization if you define them in different modules. The only thing you can be sure of is that global objects defined in the same module are initialized in their order of declaration. This book uses such an object for storing and retrieving the configuration data and calls the class *Configuration*.

Loading setup parameters from disk can lead to problems. What if the disk doesn't have the file that holds this data? The first time you run your program, the disk probably has no configuration file. You must then allow the application to run anyway, but with all parameters at their default values. Class *Configuration* takes care of this for you. Using a disk to store parameters can, however, lead to all kinds of run-time errors that must be properly handled. Chapter 14 covers device-error handling briefly.

Before looking inside the class, first consider how it fits into the application program. For convenience, this book keeps the application's setup and global configuration data in a file called *database.cpp*. The configuration object must access all pertinent variables in this file to set them up correctly. Class *Configuration* must #include the declarations for the database in its header file. This book uses a file named "DEMO.CFG" to store the data, whose format is binary. A text editor thus cannot inspect the data. This approach is the most efficient for the computer, but it doesn't help people to read the contents of the file. Some systems (such as Microsoft Windows' *win.ini* file) use an initialization file in text format. Not only are the data displayable with any ordinary text editor, but comment fields and headers are also there to make the data easy to read. This format also allows you to modify the file before running the program.

You could write class *Configuration* to support such a format by modifying its file read/write operations. Writing the data to disk in text mode is easier than reading it back, but readable text can be an advantage. Using text-configuration files slows the initialization and termination phases significantly, so you need to weigh the pros and the cons. The following listings show the header and source files for class *Configuration*.

Listing 10.1. The header file for class Configuration.

```
#ifndef CONFIGHPP
#define CONFIGHPP

#include <stdio.h>

#include "box.hpp"
#include "legend.hpp"
#include "database.hpp"

// file name of configuration parameters
#define CONFIGURATION_FILENAME "DEMO.CFG"

class Configuration {

    FILE *fp;

    void UseConfigurationFile();
    void UseDefaults();

public:

    Configuration();
    ~Configuration();
};

#endif
```

Listing 10.2. The implementation of class Configuration.

```
#include "config.hpp"

Configuration::Configuration()
{
    // load the configuration data from disk
    if ( (fp = fopen(CONFIGURATION_FILENAME,
                     "r") ) != NULL)
      UseConfigurationFile();
    else
      UseDefaults();
}


Configuration::~Configuration()
{
    // set up an error box, just in case
    BOX_TYPE box;
    box. x1 = 100;
    box. y1 = 100;
    box. x2 = 300;
```

Listing 10.2 Continues

Listing 10.2 Continued

```
                box. y2 = 200;
                Legend error_message;

                // save the configuration data to disk
                if ( (fp = fopen(CONFIGURATION_FILENAME,
                            "w") ) == NULL)
                   error_message. Center(&box, BRIGHT_RED,
                     "Can't save settings");

                // attempt to write all the settings
                if (fwrite(&RecorderSettings,
                   sizeof(RecorderData), 1, fp) != 1)

                   // something went wrong
                   error_message. Center(&box, BRIGHT_RED,
                     "Can't save settings");
            }

        void Configuration::UseConfigurationFile()
        {
                // attempt to read all the settings
                if (fread(&RecorderSettings,
                        sizeof(RecorderData), 1, fp) != 1)

                   // disk doesn't have them
                   UseDefaults();
        }

        void Configuration::UseDefaults()
        {
                RecorderData *recorder_dp = &RecorderSettings;
                recorder_dp->tape_state = 0;
                recorder_dp->fader = 0.5;
                recorder_dp->signal_level = 0;
                recorder_dp->bass = 0.5;
                recorder_dp->treble = 0.5;
                recorder_dp->source = 0;
                recorder_dp->defeat = 0;
        }
```

Function Descriptions

Configuration::Configuration

The class constructor tries to locate the configuration file in the current directory. If the file is found, it is used; otherwise default values initialize the system.

Configuration::~Configuration

Terminating the program invokes the class destructor, which tries to save the current values for all the settings in the configuration file. If unsuccessful, it displays an error message in the center of the screen. Such problems as a full disk or an open diskette door (for floppies) can cause errors.

Configuration::UseConfigurationFile

This function reads the binary data from the configuration file directly into the structure containing the application program's global data. The function attempts to detect invalid configuration files by the return value of the *fread* function. If something has gone wrong, the function assumes it got bad data and uses default values.

Configuration::UseDefaults

Default values control all the global variables for the system. The *Configuration* object thus needs both the application data declarations and the data itself.

Advantages of Automatic Configuration Files

The name of the configuration file used in class *Configuration* is fixed. Some systems elect to use several different names or to have the user input the name of it. The Integrated Development Environment of Turbo C++ itself uses the latter approach. When you start the program by typing **tc** at the DOS command prompt, Turbo C++ looks in the current directory for *.prj files. If it finds only one, it assumes that it's your project file and automatically loads it. If it finds more than one, then it doesn't know which one to use, so it loads nothing. In this situation you can type at the DOS command prompt

```
>tc myproj.prj
```

and Turbo C++ will use that project file to start up. Turbo C++ project files are nothing more than configuration files. In the preceding DOS example, several configuration files can be used according to the data to be acquired or the test being performed.

Another possibility is having the configuration file identify the version of the software used to produce it by recording this data along with the data. Too often users find themselves with disks of data written with an old version of a program, only to discover much later that they have since upgraded to a new version of software not compatible with the old data.

11

Deriving New Objects

The objects described so far are for general use, and you can build many kinds of control applications using just them. But, as always, some situations require different objects or ones with slightly different behaviors. Here the power of C++ comes to your aid, allowing the easy creation of new objects from previous ones. In a class hierarchy, you should reuse as much code as possible, "re-inventing the wheel" only as a last resort. The more complex the object you derive a new one from, the more power you et with a given amount of extra code.

Any object designed to be used with a mouse or touch-panel must be linked into the display list. The best way to do this is via the class *Icon*. Using *Icon* as a base class allows the display-list processing to be handled automatically, even if you create a new class several levels down in the inheritance tree from *Icon*. Not all objects require mouse support, so these don't need to be derived from *Icon*. The classes *Events*, *RandomNumber*, and *Legend* are in this category.

This chapter explores making new controls that satisfy specific requirements. It shows how to derive objects from both complex and simple icons and how straightforward, even repetitive, the derivation of new classes is.

Example 1: A Musical Button

With few exceptions (notably the NeXT computer), sound is greatly underrated on computers. Most systems limit their acoustic expressions to monotonic beeps. You can make a button that issues a note at a given pitch while it's pressed. Using a series of these, you can create a simple music keyboard and play it with the mouse.

Because this chapter deals with deriving objects from others, the musical button won't be designed from scratch. Using the class *MonostablePushButton* as a base class makes the design a snap. All that's left is to decide what features to add or to change, and how. Because the buttons generate sound, the only addition is the sound part itself. The event handler in Chapter 1 already contains provisions for issuing sounds at any given frequency, so this feature is all that's needed.

A class called *ToneButton* implements the new button, whose constructor expects a screen coordinate and the name of the note to generate. The screen coordinate indicates the location of the button's lower left corner on the screen. Other variables are transparently passed as necessary to the base class *Icon*. Listing 11.1 shows the header file of class *ToneButton*. The enum NOTE lists the notes available. This book uses the music notation DO-RE-MI rather than C-D-E for clarity. (The letter 'C' is particularly confusing in a book that deals with C and C++.)

The implementation of *ToneButton* shown in this section supports only a single octave, but it is not difficult to provide support for multi-octave buttons. You can see a complete octave of musical buttons in the demo program on the companion disk, on the page *Games*.

Listing 11.1. The header file for class ToneButton.

```
#ifndef TONEHPP
#define TONEHPP

#include <string.h>

#include "pushbut.hpp"
#include "events.hpp"

enum NOTE {DO, DO_SHARP,
        RE, RE_SHARP,
        MI,
        FA, FA_SHARP,
        SOL, SOL_SHARP,
        LA, LA_SHARP,
        TI
};
```

```
typedef struct s {
  char*    note_name;
  int      note_pitch;
} NOTE_DATA;


class ToneButton: public MonostablePushButton {

protected:

    NOTE note;
    int key_state;

public:

    ToneButton(int, int, NOTE);
    void LeftButtonPressed();
    void LeftButtonReleased();
};

#endif
```

Listing 11.2. *The implementation of class* ToneButton.

```
#include "tone.hpp"

static NOTE_DATA notes [] = {
  "DO",    532,
  "DO#",   554,
  "RE",    587,
  "RE#",   622,
  "MI",    659,
  "FA",    698,
  "FA#",   740,
  "SOL",   784,
  "SOL#",  831,
  "LA",    880,
  "LA#",   932,
  "TI",    988
};


ToneButton::ToneButton(int x, int y, NOTE key) :

    MonostablePushButton(x, y, "", 0, 0)
{
    // save the note
    note = key;

    // look up the name of the note and save it
    strcpy(legend, notes [note]. note_name);
```

Listing 11.2 Continues

187

Listing 11.2 Continued

```
        // pass a state variable to the base class
        key_state = 0; state = &key_state;
}

void ToneButton::LeftButtonPressed()
{
    MonostablePushButton::LeftButtonPressed();
    EventsHandler->SoundOn(notes [note]. note_pitch);
}

void ToneButton::LeftButtonReleased()
{
    EventsHandler->SoundOff();
    MonostablePushButton::LeftButtonReleased();
}
```

The file begins with a static array linking together a note's printable name with its frequency expressed in Hertz. The frequency or pitch has been rounded to the nearest integer.

Function Descriptions

ToneButton::ToneButton

The class constructor takes only three arguments but needs to pass five to the base class. The constructor passes the first three immediately; it uses nulls for the other two. The class does not need the activation function pointer, but it does require a pointer to the button state. In fact, all objects derived from class *PushButton* must have a state-variable pointer in the argument list of their base-class constructors. Normally the application program manipulates this variable. There is no application program for *ToneButton*, but the variable is nevertheless required. To simplify the creation of objects of type *ToneButton*, the state-variable pointer was dropped from the constructor's argument list. The base class, however, requires a valid state-variable pointer, so the last line of code in the constructor sets the pointer `state` in *PushButton* to point to a special protected variable `key_state`, defined in class *ToneButton*. The constructor uses the `note` parameter passed to it to look up the printable name for the button; then it stores the name in a local character array `legend`, declared `protected` in the parent class *PushButton*.

ToneButton::LeftButtonPressed

Calling the base-class equivalent function switches the button's color, setting its state to *active*, and then the note sounds. The note lasts until you release the mouse button.

ToneButton::LeftButtonReleased

This function invokes the base class to restore the color and state of the button to the inactive values. It turns off the button's tone first to prevent annoying acoustical delays on slow computers due to the display processing.

Example 2: Computer Die

Playing games of chance is nothing new for computers. Systems play anything from roulette to blackjack to poker. To keep things simple, this example shows how to make the equivalent of a die. The demo program on the companion disk shows a computer die on the page *Games*.

All games of chance make use of pseudo- or real random numbers, so first you need to build a random-number generator independent of operating system and C++ implementations. The following two listings show such a device, realized by a class called *RandomNumber*.

Listing 11.3. The header file for class RandomNumber.

```
#ifndef RANDOMHPP
#define RANDOMHPP

#include <stdlib.h>
#include "events.hpp"

class RandomNumber {

    float last_value;

public:

    RandomNumber();
    float NextValue();
};

#endif
```

Listing 11.4. The implementation of class RandomNumber.

```
#include "random.hpp"

RandomNumber::RandomNumber()
{
    // use the system time to seed the random
    // number generator
    srand(EventsHandler->SystemTime() );
}


float RandomNumber::NextValue()
{
    int value = rand();

    // convert to range (0..1)
    return (float) value / 32767;
}
```

Function Descriptions

RandomNumber::RandomNumber

The class constructor reads the system time and uses it as a seed value for the number generator. This procedure ensures that you do not use the same pseudorandom sequence each time you create a random number. The function *srand()* is an ANSI C standard function, so it should be present in most systems. The class structure of random numbers allows you to create and manipulate the numbers without worrying about this initialization step.

RandomNumber::NextValue

This function computes the next number in a pseudorandom sequence, using the ANSI C standard function *rand()*, which returns a value in the range 0..32767. To handle more general problems, this number is converted to a floating point number in the range (0..1). The degree of "randomness" of *NextValue* depends on the quality of the *rand()* function. Few implementations realize an ideal rectangular probability function, but solutions to that problem lie beyond the scope of this book.

Implementation of the Die

The ability to generate pseudo-random numbers is only the first step in building a computerized die. I will implement the die itself using a push-button as a support object. The number displayed on the push-button represents the result of the last roll of the die. Clicking the push-button makes the die go rapidly through a pseudo-random sequence. The sequencing continues until the button is released, and while the numbers cycle, the push-button appears in a highlighted color to show that the die is rolling. The following listing shows the header for class *Die*.

Listing 11.5. The header file for class Die.

```
#ifndef DIEHPP
#define DIEHPP

#include "pushbut.hpp"
#include "random.hpp"
#include "events.hpp"

class Die: public MonostablePushButton {

    int frequency;
    void MakeSound();
    void GetNextRoll();

protected:

    int die_state;
    RandomNumber value;
    int current_roll;

public:

    Die(int, int);
    virtual void Update();
};

#endif
```

The two private functions *GetNextRoll( )* and *MakeSound( )* are used by the other member functions of *Die*, and are not accessible outside the class. The function *MakeSound( )* emits a sound that resembles the kind heard in video arcades. Because the sound pitch changes each time the function is called, the variable `frequency` is used to save the value between function calls. The class variable value supports the random-sequencing feature of the die, and `current_roll` holds the integer value of the last roll. Creating an object of class Die automatically randomizes the pseudo-random sequence. Listing 11.6 shows the class implementation.

Listing 11.6. The implementation of class Die.

```
#include "die.hpp"

Die::Die(int x, int y) :
    MonostablePushButton(x, y, "", 0, 0)
{
    // establish a state variable for the icon
    die_state = 0;
    state = &die_state;

    // set the roll sound pitch
    frequency = 300;

    // roll the die once
    GetNextRoll();
}
```

```
void Die::GetNextRoll()
{
    // roll the die again
    float random = value.NextValue();

    // convert to integer in the range (1..6)
    current_roll = (random * 6) + 1;

    // convert to ascii for the button legend
    sprintf(legend, "%d", current_roll);
}

void Die::MakeSound()
{
    // make a short sound
    EventsHandler->SoundOn(frequency, 5);

    // change the pitch for next time
    frequency += 100;
    if (frequency == 1000) frequency = 300;
}

void Die::Update()
{
    if (*state == 0) return;
    // compute the next value of the die
    GetNextRoll();

    // issue a brief "computer" sound
    MakeSound();

    // turn off mouse so THAT the die doesn't
    // obscure it
    EventsHandler->HideMouseCursor();
```

```
                    // show the new value of the die
                    Display();

                    // put mouse cursor back on top of die
                    EventsHandler->ShowMouseCursor();
      }
```

Function Descriptions

Die::Die

The constructor's simple interface requires only the specification of the screen coordinates. The base class *MonostablePushButton* receives a null legend string along with a null activation function. The latter is not necessary, because icons of class *Die* interact with the user directly on the screen. The base class *MonostablePushButton* requires a pointer to an integer state-variable. This variable stores the current active/inactive state of the button. Because the constructor for class *Die* received no such pointer, you must establish one in the body of the constructor code. The state-variable pointer `state` is defined in the parent class *PushButton*, and it is set to point to the variable `die_state`, declared `protected` in class *Die*.

To conclude, the newly created die is rolled. Note that the constructor shows nothing on the screen.

Die::GetNextRoll

This private function computes the next value in a pseudorandom sequence, converts it to an integer between one and six; then it converts it to printable format. This function does not update the screen.

Die::MakeSound

This private function issues a 5-millisecond beep. The frequency changes in 100 Hz increments each time you invoke the function, and rapid sequencing recreates a "computer sound."

Die::Update

This function is the same one used earlier to support animation. Rolling a die can be considered a form of animation because the die changes its appearance continuously. The screen handler invokes the *Update()* function for all icons in the display list, to keep them animated. Most icons will have no *Update()* function of their own, and thus will do nothing, but class *Die* is different. Clicking the die switches it temporarily to an active state, during which animation is enabled. The *Update()* function then takes over and rolls the die. Each time the function is executed, a new sound pitch is computed and emitted.

Example 3: A Lotto Card Randomizer

Many countries have popular games of chance such as lotteries and lottos. The rules are just about as simple as they can get. The ticket price is low and the winnings are sometimes enormous, a combination that attracts people by the millions. In the state of California, the lotto had 49 numbers (until recently). You have to pick six numbers when you buy a ticket. If your numbers match those picked by a state representative, you win the jackpot. This example develops a simple object that generates the six numbers required for a lotto card. In keeping with the theme of the chapter, the example derives the object from one already implemented. The only shortcoming in the implementation shown here: the six numbers generated might not differ from each other. It's simple to correct this problem, and it is left as an exercise to the reader.

The lotto card needs to display a set of six numbers chosen at random. This suggests using a compound object, in which a single parent icon coordinates the actions of six child icons. The parent could compute all the random numbers and send a message to each child to display these numbers. A lotto card could be displayed as six buttons side-by-side, suggesting the use of *HorizontalSelector* as a base class. With this implementation, the lotto card will look like the one in figure 11.1. A real object of class *Lotto* can be seen in the demo program supplied on the companion disk, on page Games.

Fig. 11.1. The lotto card.

To make a *Lotto* object display a new set of randomly chosen numbers, there must be a way of interacting with the user. The class described here computes new numbers when clicked with the mouse, and this is easily accomplished by overriding the *LeftButtonPressed( )* and *LeftButtonReleased( )* functions of the base class *Icon*.

To make the object more appealing, class *Lotto* was designed to issue a sequence of computer sounds while clicked, and all buttons display a ? character. The function *Lotto::Select( )* determines how a selector behaves when one of its buttons is clicked. Overriding this function allows you to modify the default behavior. Class *Lotto* lets you click on each of its six buttons, and responds by highlighting the button clicked.

After the characteristics of the *Lotto* class have been decided, the implementation is rather straightforward. The class is designed to use a compound base class to make use of code already written and debugged. User classes should always be written to take advantage of other classes if possible. The generic procedure for designing a new class is to first determine what the class will do, then how it will behave, and finally how it will be used. All this will be reflected in the public interface of the class. Listing 11.7 shows the header file for class *Lotto*.

Listing 11.7. The header file for class Lotto.

```
#ifndef LOTTOHPP
#define LOTTOHPP

#include <string.h>

#include "selector.hpp"
#include "random.hpp"
#include "legend.hpp"

#define MAX_LOTTO_BUTTONS 6

class Lotto: public HorizontalSelector {

        int lotto_state;
        int number;
```

Listing 11.2 Continues

Listing 11.7 Continued

```
            RandomNumber value;
            void Refresh();
            void Clear();
            void MakeSound();
            int NextPick();

    public:

            Lotto(int, int);
            void Update();
            void LeftButtonPressed();
            void LeftButtonReleased();
    };

    #endif
```

The *RandomNumber* class generates each number on the card. When you create the lotto card object, the random number generator is automatically initialized and ready to go.

Next are four private functions, which provide support to functions in the public interface. Listing 11.8 shows the complete implementation of the class.

Listing 11.8. The implementation of class Lotto.

```
    #include "lotto.hpp"

    Lotto::Lotto(int x, int y) :

            HorizontalSelector(x, y,
            "Lotto Ticket Randomizer",
            0, 0, "", "", "", "", "", "")

    {
        // set the object state to inactive
        lotto_state = 0;

        // don't let any buttons get highlighted
        number = -1;
        button_selected = &number;

        // show the first random picks
        Refresh();
    }

    void Lotto::LeftButtonPressed()
    {
        // switch to active state so that the Update()
        // function takes control
        lotto_state = 1;
```

```
      // hide all pick numbers
      Clear();

      // highlight all the buttons
      for (int i = 0; i < MAX_LOTTO_BUTTONS; i++)
        button [i]->Highlight();
}


void Lotto::LeftButtonReleased()
{
      // switch to inactive state
      lotto_state = 0;

      // look up the next pick series
      Refresh();
      Display();

      // unhighlight all the buttons
      for (int i = 0; i < MAX_LOTTO_BUTTONS; i++)
        button [i]->UnHighlight();
}

int Lotto::NextPick()
{
      // roll the die again
      float random = value.NextValue();

      // convert to integer in the range (1..49)
      return (random * 49) + 1;
}

void Lotto::Clear()
{
      // refresh all the pick numbers
      for (int i = 0; i < MAX_LOTTO_BUTTONS; i++) {
        char string [20];
        button [i]->SetLegend("?");
      }
      Display();
}

void Lotto::Refresh()
{
      // refresh all the pick numbers
      for (int i = 0; i < MAX_LOTTO_BUTTONS; i++) {
        char string [20];
        int new_pick = NextPick();
        sprintf(string, "%d", new_pick);
        button [i]->SetLegend(string);
      }
}
```

Listing 11.8 Continues

197

Listing 11.8 Continued

```
void Lotto::MakeSound()
{
      // get a random number
      float random = value.NextValue();

      // convert to frequency in range 100..2000 Hz
      int frequency = (random * 1900) + 100;

      // make a short sound
      EventsHandler->SoundOn(frequency, 30);
}

void Lotto::Update()
{
      if (lotto_state == 0) return;
      MakeSound();
}
```

Function Descriptions

Lotto::Lotto

The class constructor receives the coordinates of the lower left corner of the lotto card and invokes the base class *HorizontalSelector* with a parameter indicating the name of the lotto card. Six null strings are also passed to the base class, and this is necessary because class *HorizontalSelector* counts the number of strings to determine the number of buttons to create on the selector.

An animation control variable in *Lotto* called `lotto_state` has a value that is initially set to zero. When the lotto object is clicked, `lotto_state` is set to 1, which in turns enables the animation function *Lotto:Update()* to take over to issue the computer sounds.

The variable `number` is not used directly in class *Lotto*, but is required by the base class. The value of `number` indicates which button of the selector to highlight. Setting the value of this variable to (-1) ensures that no button will be highlighted.

Lotto::LeftButtonPressed

Clicking a non-child area of the object executes this function. The area includes the button legend area and the spaces between the buttons. The function sets the ticket state to one, enabling the *Update* function to erase all buttons and display ? characters on highlighted fields.

Lotto:LeftButtonReleased

This function deactivates the object, showing a new set of pick numbers. The buttons are returned to their inactive color.

Lotto::NextPick

This private function returns a random number in the range (1..49). It uses the random number generator object `value` for all the work.

Lotto::Clear

This private function erases the previous pick numbers and displays a ? character on all buttons.

Lotto::Refresh

This private function computes the next set of pick numbers for the lotto ticket but does not modify the screen.

Lotto::MakeSound

This private function issues a 30-millisecond beep at a frequency randomly selected between 100 and 2000 Hz.

Lotto::Update

Class *Screen* invokes this function to support animation. This object uses animation to issue sounds, not to move around on the screen. The function lies dormant when the object is inactive. Executing *LeftButtonPressed* sets the `lotto_state` variable to the value 1, causing the sound generator to wake up and issue a sequence of random sounds. The sounds last until *LeftButtonReleased* is executed, when you let go of the mouse button.

12

The Application-Interface Connection

Your first computer programs are simple ones that do one thing, such as displaying the message `"Hello, world!"` on-screen. You then create more complex programs until you master the programming language. You study programs written by others to learn techniques, but you focus on details of implementation. To build your first project, you always follow the same procedure: studying the problem to be solved and writing a program to solve it. This method structures most computer-science courses.

What's wrong with this approach? You started the project from the application and did not deal with the user until you needed input or output. This approach is like designing the inside of a house and building it, starting on the interior design. After putting the walls around the furnished rooms, you paint their exterior. If you change your mind about the location of a wall, you have to tear up the carpeting, scrap the wallpaper, move all the furniture, relocate the wall, and decorate the room again.

The best way to proceed with a software project is to consider how the program is going to be used and how it will *look*. Most software programs are too complicated to be designed from scratch in one swoop. Using early prototypes of a program, you get a better feel for the various events that take place when the system is running.

Rapid prototyping is an excellent way to start a large project. Using screen layout tools or even PAINT programs, you make a series of screen snapshots that show the system display in its salient states. Some tools, such as the *Interface Design Tool* (IDT) from Ithaca Software Systems, Inc., allow you to generate C initialization code directly from screen layouts. Dan Bricklin's DEMO II program, distributed by Sage Software Inc., allows you to use a series of captured screens to interact directly with the developer. By pressing keys you can make the screen change any way you like, thus simulating a finished product with surprising effectiveness.

The important thing at this stage is to put every effort toward designing the user interface first, based on the early notions of what the application program do when implemented. You should write little or no code; spend your time studying and enhancing the effectiveness of the interface, not of the implementation details of the coding. Heavy use of commercial prototyping tools is beneficial.

This *interface-first* method is valuable for projects of all sizes. Programmers usually refine designs after the prototyping phase, but the most dramatic changes come early in project development, when the understanding of a product's functions is still sketchy.

This method also tends to create greater consistency in the interface, which makes a program easier to use. Knowing what interface constructs (such as dialog boxes, list boxes, and buttons) are available from the start makes it more unlikely for an application to "invent" a new one when dealing with a nonstandard case. It is easier to either modify the application details to conform or to use a combination of standard constructs.

Most Programs Have Things in Common

Certain basic phrases in our vocabulary are fundamental. No matter what we talk about, we need to use them. Computer programs are similar, whether we're writing word-processing, database management, spreadsheet, process control, or data-communications programs. The following is a sampling of such fundamentals:

- File reading and writing

- Keyboard handling

- Screen handling

- Mouse handling

- Directory handling

- Menus

- Windows

- Editing

Many of these are related to the user interface, and yet people continue to re-solve the same problems with every project. Although no two projects have the same requirements, their interfaces shouldn't have to be reinvented every time. Thus a single interface could be designed to handle a variety of applications.

System Architectures

It's time to step back from the implementation details for a moment to study the overall structure of GUIs. By comparing different approaches, you can appreciate the pros and cons of each.

This book deals with systems that are single-tasking, connected to a single display monitor, and controlled by a mouse and keyboard. Normally multiple popup windows or pages organize the multitude of controls required. I encourage using touch-sensitive screens for many applications, because they remove that extra level of mouse complexity from commands. Adding a multitasking capability to an interface is not difficult if you limit yourself to the nonpreemptive type. Take a look at the overall architecture for the typical system described throughout this book.

This system is not a pure *event driven* one. The top-level module function has a so-called event loop, where the system checks for event activity, calling the event handler when necessary. The handler determines which icon to send the event to. This icon thus has the *input focus* for that action, and it is invoked.

You can endow icons with an activation function, triggered when you activate or deactivate the icon. The Open Software Foundation's *Motif* GUI allows widgets (the equivalent of this book's icons) to possess multiple activation functions, denoted as callback functions or simply *callbacks*. This simplifies them because each one handles only a narrow range of events—often only one.

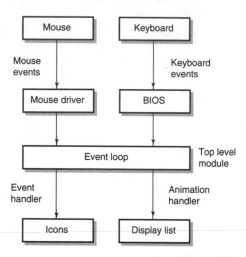

Fig. 12.1. The connection between user and icons.

In a truly event-driven system, the interface essentially stops running between events and simply waits or performs housekeeping routines. A mouse or keyboard action causes an interrupt that directly invokes the function to process it. These systems have two distinct levels that act as virtual machines or processes running asynchronously with respect to each other. The idle process is the *background* and the event process is the *foreground*.

This architecture is different from many popular systems, such as X Windows, Microsoft Windows, and the Apple MACINTOSH. These support a nonpreemptive multitasking structure with a simple technique. To run an application, you must furnish it with its own event loop, with continuous calls to the interface handler.

The following listing is a C code fragment illustrating the event loop in an application under X Windows.

Listing 12.1. The event loop under X Windows.

```
/* application's event loop */
while (1) {
  /* give control to X Windows */
  XNextEvent(display, &event);

  /* event detected: process it */
  switch (event. type) {
```

```
    /* dispatch the proper handling function */
    case ...:
    case ...:
    case ...:
  }
}
```

When running under Microsoft Windows, the event loop is similar to the one shown in listing 12.1. Windows is more extensive than X Windows, because it is a complete GUI supporting more than windowing functions and event handlers. In my view, however, X Windows is an improvement because it isolates the windowing functions from the user-interface layer. The code fragment in listing 12.2 shows the application program's event loop under Windows.

Listing 12.2. The event loop under Microsoft Windows.

```
/* stay in this loop until Windows returns 0 */
while (GetMessage(&msg, NULL, 0, 0) ) {

  /* select a handler based on the event type */
  DispatchMessage(&msg);

}

/* terminate the application */
. . .
```

Using events loops like these, the interface is in control between events. It can thus invoke in a round-robin fashion all the active applications, simulating time-sliced multitasking. The method has drawbacks, however, listed here:

1. It works only for well-behaved applications that don't "hog" the system. If an application decides to execute a 20-minute routine without calling the interface periodically, the multitasking shuts down until it's done.

2. Every application must duplicate the same basic event loop. Not only is this a waste of code, but it also complicates the application, with the added risk of losing system control if an application is ill-behaved or crashes.

3. This method removes system-control features, such as determining when to terminate a program, from the top-level interface and buries them inside each application. Inconsistencies and a greater probability of bugs and system crashes during program development result.

The Top-Level Module

The GUI described in this book is a stand-alone system, meaning the interface is compiled and linked to the application at development time. Many commercial systems work this way, like MetaWindow by Metagraphics Software Corp. On the contrary, systems such as NextStep or Motif are dynamically connected to application programs at run-time.

The previous chapters concentrated on specific objects in the GUI, but you did not learn how to *run* them or how to tie everything together. You need to write a top-level module that takes control when you run the program. The module must initialize the system, create all the necessary objects, coordinate the event handler, etc. Using C++, this book emphasizes classes. Consequently the *main()* function for the GUI is short. Actually, listing 12.3 shows its coding exactly.

Listing 12.3. The GUI's main() function.

```
#include "config.hpp"
#include "top.hpp"

Configuration Setup;
TopLevel control;

main() {}
```

There's *nothing* to it[md]literally. So how does it work? The answer is that the main function doesn't do anything. That inconspicuous declaration of the global variable control runs the system. The variable is an instance of the class *TopLevel*, whose constructor has all the code for running the system. Listing 12.4 shows the files for *Toplevel*.

Listing 12.4. The header file for class TopLevel.

```
#ifndef TOPLEVELHPP
#define TOPLEVELHPP

#include "screen.hpp"
#include "graphics.hpp"
#include "listmgr.hpp"
#include "events.hpp"
#include "applic.hpp"


class TopLevel {
```

```
public:
    TopLevel();
};

#endif
```

Listing 12.5. The implementation of class TopLevel.

```
#include "top.hpp"
#include "applic.hpp"

TopLevel::TopLevel()

{
    // load the graphics handler
    GraphicsHandler = new Graphics;

    // initialize and display the basic screen area
    CurrentScreen = new Screen;
    CurrentScreen->DisplayTemplate();

    // create the application-specific objects
    CreateApplication();

    // load the event handler
    EventsHandler = new Events;
    EventsHandler->ShowMouseCursor();

    // wait for operator commands and process them
    while {
        EventsHandler->ProcessMouseActions();
        EventsHandler->ProcessUserKeys();
        CurrentScreen->Update();
        RunApplication();
    }
}
```

The first thing in running the GUI is to initialize all the application variables. I keep them in the file *database.cpp* and declare them in *database.hpp*. Declaring the global object *Setup* in the top-level module guarantees initialization of the system variables before calling the *main* function. When the application terminates, you can endow *TopLevel* objects with a destructor to handle any cleanup operations.

You must set up the graphics handler before creating any additional objects, in case error messages need to be displayed by the system. This puts the system into graphics mode and establishes a handler for all screen output. Next comes creating the screen handler and the basic screen template. Many systems use a common format for all screens and fit the controls into common areas. This gives users instant familiarity when switching pages or applications and allows constant display of such items as company logos or project-version numbers without getting the application involved. GUIs from different manufacturers have their own look and feel. They can be recognized immediately on the screen by their templates.

Now it's time to connect the interface to the application. You can use the *CreateApplication* function to start up processes not intended for control of the page selector. Simple applications, which might have only one display to show, do away with the page selector entirely.

In typical systems with multiple pages, editing the global array *Pages* inserts references to the pages to be activated. Each reference creates an application-specific page and displays it by calling a single-member function of an application page. For simpler cases, such as the one in listing 12.6, you need to just create and display the objects necessary.

Listing 12.6. The function creating an application consisting of a single lotto randomizer ticket.

```
#include "lotto.hpp"

void CreateApplication()
{
    Lotto* lotto = new Lotto(200, 120);
    lotto->Display();
}
```

The location for *CreateApplication* in the module *applic.cpp* isolates any changes from the top-level module, which should be application-independent. Always relegate functions that depend on the setup, the application, the hardware, or other items to specific modules for easy development, maintenance, and porting. Chapter 14 deals with the issue of dependency insulation in detail.

After the application, the event handler is created. The event loop then captures all user actions and dispatches them into the application program. This loop also controls icon animation through a single call to *Screen::Update*, which searches through the display list and activates the *Update* function for every icon in the application. Few icons are animated, so the process means repeatedly calling the null virtual function *Update* in class *Icon*. The loop time here is highly variable, depending on the number of icons created, the amount of processing needed to animate them, and the speed of the hardware. A refinement could be scheduling the updating of each animated icon at given times or even subdividing the various icons into different levels of priority if the hardware can't keep up with the system requirements.

The last function is *RunApplication*. In a traditional non-GUI system it corresponds to the *main* function as the starting point for the entire system. Although it seems to have only marginal significance here, it actually keeps the application "alive" in the absence of user input.

For example, a program using a MIDI interface to control musical instruments might need to capture the events, showing them on the screen in graphical format. A process-control system needs to poll all remote sensors to keep its internal database up to date. A cockpit-control panel needs to poll all the flight sensors constantly to show the current parameters to the pilot.

Some programs do not need *RunApplication* at all, like one of those DOS shells that display a graphical directory tree and allow the user to make selections with a mouse. When the user is idle, the program has nothing to do.

You add *RunApplication* to the file *applic.cpp* along with *CreateApplication* to insulate the application-dependent code from the system. An alternative to using C functions for the application is creating a class called *Application*, whose member variables consist of the application objects and whose constructor is responsible for creating and displaying the objects.

The Event Path for Mouse Actions

Knowing how the pieces go together doesn't show exactly how they work. Figure 12.1 gives a rough idea. It's time to be specific.

As stated, the program spends most of its time in the event loop inside class *TopLevel*. Pressing a mouse button calls the function *Events::ProcessMouseActions*. The following shows the complete path followed when dealing with a left mouse button click, starting from the top-level event loop:

1. Event loop

2. Events::ProcessMouseActions

3. Screen::LeftButtonChanged

4. Icon::LeftButtonPressed

If the button is down while you drag the mouse, *Events::ProcessMouseActions* notifies the currently selected icon (if any) directly. The event handler does not know the icon's fate. If you don't drag the mouse with the button down, *Screen::LeftButtonChanged* is called. This function handles both button pressing and releasing. The first thing it does is determine which icon you clicked. It traverses the display list backward, searching for the first icon that occupies the screen coordinate you clicked. If it finds an icon, its member function Icon::LeftButtonPressed is called; otherwise, the GUI ignores the mouse event. Releasing the left mouse button causes similar processing.

The Event Path for Keyboard Actions

The keys on a computer keyboard can generate different kinds of events, but this book only has one function to deal with the keyboard, called *Icon::KeyTyped( )*. When a key is typed, the icon with the input focus uses *Icon::KeyTyped( )* to process the event. Not all keyboard actions are handled, such as releasing a key, auto-repeating a key, and pressing the Caps Lock key.

When a keyboard event is detected, some object in the GUI must be found to handle it, and the icon with the input focus will be selected. If no icon has the input focus, the key event is ignored. The GUI described in this book requires you to click on an icon in order to give it the input focus. The following shows the complete path followed when dealing with a keystroke, starting from the top-level event loop:

1. Event loop

2. Events::ProcessUserKeys

3. Screen::KeyTyped

4. Icon::KeyTyped

In this book most icons accept only mouse events, because I deal mainly with systems designed for commands and controls, not databases and word processing. When *Screen::KeyTyped* finds the targeted icon and invokes *Icon::KeyTyped*, it doesn't know how the key is handled or whether the icon can even handle keystrokes. The null-virtual function *Icon::KeyTyped* allows the system to work normally without this knowledge.

13

Putting It All Together

A complete application program, representing a virtual tape recorder, illustrates the simplicity and power of an object-oriented programming approach. The term *virtual* means it works like a recorder without actually using one. This chapter uses new objects derived from ones previously described. Using inheritance simplifies the job, reducing the coding to a minimum.

Polymorphism specializes the behavior of derived classes with little impact on the structure of the overall program. This book makes extensive use of it for displaying objects, handling mouse clicks, and supporting animation.

Showing a sample application program is challenging because its level of complexity has to be just right. If it's too simple, it doesn't drive home all the concepts. If it's too complex, the book becomes a description of a specific case. This chapter uses a problem that employs most of the programming techniques shown and yet requires only limited code. Its purpose is proving the general-purpose nature of the graphical user interface described and to show how easily you can tailor it to your own needs.

The Application

Everybody knows what a piano keyboard looks like. Today you can buy simple electronic keyboards with internal memory. Pressing a button allows you to record melodies and play them back later. This chapter describes a computer analog of this instrument, using the mouse to play, record, and playback. The recorder has the usual controls of a tape recorder, including a *tape counter*, which indicates how far along the recorder is in a melody. The fast-forward and rewind buttons move you quickly to any point. Rewinding stops automaticaly when the counter reaches zero. The fast-forward button stops when the counter reaches the "end of the tape."

Although there is no actual magnetic tape involved, the system simulates it well. During playback, the counter wraps back around to zero at the tape's end, allowing a tune to be played repeatedly by itself. The companion disk has the complete program. Selecting the page *Piano* in the demo program runs it.

The program's limitations are strictly acoustic. The keyboard allows only monophonic melodies, which means you can play only one key at a time. You cannot play regular chords using a mouse, but perhaps you could with a touch screen, although most touch systems don't allow multiple points to be touched simultaneously. The primitive sound circuitry in most personal computers makes creating polyphonic music difficult. A NeXT workstation solves this problem with utmost elegance, supporting full polyphonic stereo digital audio.

Another problem is the crudeness of the sounds produced. On IBM-compatible personal computers, sound generates through a small speaker whose main purpose is emitting beeps. A mediocre square-wave audio signal produces this kind of sound. Playing the keyboard thus generates square waves of different frequencies.

The application shown here stores melodies not permanently on disk, but in a memory buffer allocated dynamically. Terminating the program loses all melodies stored. Adding disk support for the melodies is fairly simple, but this section focuses on a few selected topics instead. The chapter dealing with the configuration object shows how to save objects and retrieve them automatically to and from disk when you run an application.

Figure 13.1 shows what the screen looks like when selecting the *Piano* page in the demo program.

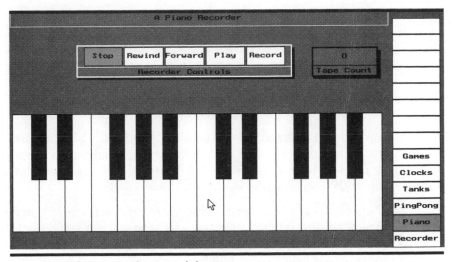

Fig. 13.1. The screen layout of the Piano *page.*

Although there are three objects shown, the program needs a fourth one, which is not displayed. The icons displayed are those used to control the piano recorder. The one *not* shown actually stores and plays the melodies.

The source of the sound to be recorded is the piano keyboard. To play it, merely click on its keys with the mouse. The PC's timer chip generates the sound, emitted for as long as you hold the key. This characteristic makes the keyboard behave more like an organ than a piano, because of the notes' indefinite sustaining capability. The following sections show how to design the necessary objects.

A General Purpose Keyboard

The first icon described is also the most complicated. Consider the overall design process before looking at source code. The most basic object is one capable of making sound. Class *ToneButton* described such an object previously, but here you need something more refined. You need not one but twelve icons to create a full octave of sound. In fact you need the option of creating any arbitrary octave of piano keys so you can place them next to each other and give the impression of a single keyboard.

The keyboard icon needed should be kept as simple and generic as possible, using a divide-et-impera strategy. The class obviously must be capable of making sound, but no provisions should be made for using the sound in any way. The class should be designed to be extended by derived classes.

213

Such a keyboard can be designed in two basic ways: as a single complex object or as set of simpler child icons linked together by a parent compound object. Given the choice, it is always better to use the second approach. The piano keys are the child icons, and they have a common object as a parent to coordinate the key activity. The overall keyboard object that results is slightly unusual because the parent object is not displayed—only the children are.

A keyboard has two kinds of keys: white and black. Should a separate class be designed for each type of key or not? The answer is subjective, but I always try to keep the number of classes to a minimum to avoid winding up with too many files and replication of code.

This chapter uses the class *PianoKey* to represent any key on a keyboard. The class constructor is told the size, location, color, and pitch of the key. The header file defines all the key dimensions, both for black and white ones, as a function of the width of a white key. By changing this value you can easily scale the size of all keys up or down.

No white keys have a regular rectangular shape. This suggests a complicated program of piecewise object construction, but consider the display process of icons: those created later show up on *top* of older ones. If you make rectangular white keys and then inset the black keys between them, everything comes out right. The trick is simply to make the white keys *before* the black ones.

As for class *ToneButton*, this chapter uses the Italian DO-RE-MI notation, more commonly used throughout the world than the C-D-E one. One octave has seven white keys and five black ones. On a keyboard there is no black key between MI and FA, because there is only one semitone between them. Consequently the pitch for MI# would be the same as the FA. To keep things simple when computing pitches and displaying keys, the macro NUMBER_OF_BLACK_KEYS is set to six, which includes the non-existent MI# key, but only five keys are created. The code in listing 13.2 skips over the key corresponding to MI#.

After the *PianoKey* class definition comes the parent class *PianoKeyboard*. When you click a key, it sends a message to the parent, which is responsible for making the sound. This approach seems more flexible than making the key itself issue its note. The child icons might not know the keyboard characteristics, such as timbre, attach, sustain, and decay. Making the keyboard handle events paves the way for subsequent recording of sounds.

During keyboard creation, the class defaults to using the middle DO octave. To get different octaves, you merely specify its pitch coefficient, using middle DO as the reference octave. A value of two gets the next octave, a three the following, and so on.

The functions *KeyPressed* and *KeyReleased* in class *PianoKeyboard* have been declared virtual, so they are ready for overriding by a future object that can handle recording. The only thing they provide is the basic action of generating sound.

The class header and source code can be seen in listings 13.1 and 13.2.

Listing 13.1. The header file for class PianoKeyboard.

```
#ifndef PIANOHPP
#define PIANOHPP

#include "graphics.hpp"
#include "icon.hpp"
#include "box.hpp"

#define WHITE_KEYS_PER_OCTAVE 7

// there is no MI# note, but count it anyway to
// simplify the computation of pitch
#define BLACK_KEYS_PER_OCTAVE 6

#define KEYS_PER_OCTAVE (WHITE_KEYS_PER_OCTAVE + \
               BLACK_KEYS_PER_OCTAVE)

// relate all key dimensions to the white key width
// so keys can easily be scaled up or down without
// altering their aspect ratio

#define WHITE_KEY_WIDTH 38
#define WHITE_KEY_HEIGHT (9 * WHITE_KEY_WIDTH / 2)
#define BLACK_KEY_WIDTH (5 * WHITE_KEY_WIDTH / 8)
#define BLACK_KEY_HEIGHT (5 * WHITE_KEY_WIDTH / 2)
#define KEYBOARD_WIDTH \
    ( (WHITE_KEY_WIDTH + 1) * WHITE_KEYS_PER_OCTAVE)

class PianoKey: public Icon {

    friend class PianoKeyboard;
    PianoKeyboard* parent;
    COLOR_TYPE key_color;
    int key_frequency;
    Box* key;

public:

    PianoKey(PianoKeyboard*, int, int,
         int, int, COLOR_TYPE, int);
```

Listing 13.1 Continues

Listing 13.1 Continued

```
      void Display();
      void LeftButtonPressed();
      void LeftButtonReleased();
      ~PianoKey();
};

class PianoKeyboard: public Icon {

      PianoKey* key [KEYS_PER_OCTAVE + 1];
      void CreateWhiteKeys(int, int, int);
      void CreateBlackKeys(int, int, int);

public:

      PianoKeyboard(int, int, int octave = 1);
      void Display();
      virtual void KeyPressed(int frequency);
      virtual void KeyReleased(int frequency);
      virtual ~PianoKeyboard();
};

#endif
```

Listing 13.2. The implementation of class PianoKeyboard.

```
#include "piano.hpp"

PianoKeyboard::PianoKeyboard(int x, int y, int octave) :
      Icon(x, y,
       x + WHITE_KEY_WIDTH * WHITE_KEYS_PER_OCTAVE,
       y + WHITE_KEY_HEIGHT)
{
      // create the white keys first
      CreateWhiteKeys(x, y, octave);

      // then overlay the black keys between them
      CreateBlackKeys(x, y, octave);
}

void PianoKeyboard::CreateWhiteKeys(int x, int y, int octave)
{
      // white notes in the middle DO octave:
      // DO, RE, MI, FA, SOL, LA, TI
      static int white_notes [] = {
        532, 587, 659, 698, 784, 880, 988
      };
      int key_x;

      for (int note = 0;
           note < WHITE_KEYS_PER_OCTAVE;
           note++) {
```

```
                key_x = x + note * (WHITE_KEY_WIDTH + 1);
                key [note] = new PianoKey(this, key_x, y,
                            WHITE_KEY_WIDTH,
                            WHITE_KEY_HEIGHT,
                            WHITE, octave * white_notes [note]
        );
        }
}

void PianoKeyboard::CreateBlackKeys(int x, int y, int
octave)
{
        int key_x, key_y;
        // black notes in the middle DO octave:
        // DO#, RE#, (leave room for MI#), FA#, SOL#, LA#
        static int black_notes [] = {
          554, 622, 698, 740, 831, 932
        };
        int i, note;

        // overlay the black keys bewteen the white ones
        for (i = 0, note = WHITE_KEYS_PER_OCTAVE;
            note < KEYS_PER_OCTAVE;
            i++, note++) {

          // there's no black between MI and FA
          if (note == 9) continue;

          key_x = x + (note - WHITE_KEYS_PER_OCTAVE) *
                (WHITE_KEY_WIDTH + 1) +
                WHITE_KEY_WIDTH - BLACK_KEY_WIDTH / 2;
          key_y = y + WHITE_KEY_HEIGHT - BLACK_KEY_HEIGHT;

          key [note] = new PianoKey(this, key_x, key_y,
                            BLACK_KEY_WIDTH,
                            BLACK_KEY_HEIGHT,
                            BLACK, octave * black_notes [i] );
        }
}
void PianoKeyboard::Display()
{
        // display all the keys
        for (int note = 0; note < KEYS_PER_OCTAVE; note++) {
          // there's no black between MI and FA
          if (note == 9) continue;
          key [note] ->Display();
        }
}

void PianoKeyboard::KeyPressed(int frequency)
    {
```

Listing 13.2 Continues

217

Listing 13.2 Continued

```
        EventsHandler->SoundOn(frequency);
}

void PianoKeyboard::KeyReleased(int frequency)
{
        EventsHandler->SoundOff();
}

PianoKeyboard::~PianoKeyboard()
{
        // eliminate all the keys
        for (int note = 0; note < KEYS_PER_OCTAVE; note++)
{
          // there's no black between MI and FA
          if (note == 9) continue;
          delete key [note];
        }
}

PianoKey::PianoKey(PianoKeyboard* keyboard,
            int x, int y, int width, int height,
            COLOR_TYPE color, int frequency) :
            Icon(x, y, x + width, y + height)
{
        // save the key attributes
        parent = keyboard;
        key_color = color;
        key_frequency = frequency;

        // create the key
        key = new Box(x1, y1, width, height, color, color);
}

void PianoKey::Display()
{
        key->Display();
}

void PianoKey::LeftButtonPressed()
{
        parent->KeyPressed(key_frequency);
}

void PianoKey::LeftButtonReleased()
{
        parent->KeyReleased(key_frequency);
}

PianoKey::~PianoKey()
{
        delete key;
}
```

Function Descriptions

PianoKeyboard::PianoKeyboard

The class constructor uses two private-member functions to create all the white and black keys. The functions pass the keyboard location and dimensions to the base class *Icon* for inclusion in the display list.

PianoKeyboard::CreateWhiteKeys

This function dynamically allocates each of the seven white keys in an octave. The octave parameter computes the actual pitch for each key, which is then passed to and stored inside the *PianoKey* class.

PianoKeyboard::CreateBlackKeys

This is similar to the previous function, except that it skips MI#. Observe the note's place holder in the array *black_notes*, where its frequency is the same as FA's (698 Hz).

PianoKeyboard::Display

This function displays each of the 12 notes in a single octave. Notice how it skips MI# (which was never created). Any attempts by the parent to manipulate the MI# key would crash the system.

PianoKeyboard::KeyPressed

A child key invokes this function when you click the mouse. Only the child class *PianoKey* stores pitches, so it informs the parent what pitch to issue.

PianoKeyboard::KeyReleased

This function turns the sound generation hardware off. A child key invokes this function when you release the mouse button.

PianoKeyboard::~PianoKeyboard

The virtual class destructor relinquishes the storage used for the child icons. It invokes the base class to remove all items from the display list. It is declared virtual so that a derived class that supports recording can override it.

PianoKey::PianoKey

The class constructor saves the key's three main attributes: the identity of the parent, key color, and pitch. Note that the parent keyboard knows nothing about the pitches for each key once you create the keys. Before exiting, the constructor creates a box of the required size and color. Once displayed, this box is not repainted for the life of the object unless uncovered by a popup window. Most icons respond to mouse actions by changing color, but those of class *PianoKey* provide operator feedback by emitting sounds. The constructor itself does *not* modify the screen.

PianoKey::Display

This function paints a piano key on the screen. It does so by sending a *Display* message to the *Box* icon dynamically allocated in the constructor. This icon knows what location, size, and color to use when displaying itself.

PianoKey::LeftButtonPressed

This function can be used directly to issue sound as a response to a mouse click. For flexibility, however, this action was deferred to the parent object, which can not only issue sounds but also do anything else it wants. This insulates the structure of a *PianoKey* icon from the applications in which the parent keyboard is used. The parent is invoked with the pitch of the note to issue, because the parent otherwise would not know which button was being handled.

PianoKey::LeftButtonReleased

The details of this function are similar to the preceding one. This function also calls the parent to handle the event, and passes an argument indicating the pitch to turn off. This argument is not required in systems capable of issuing only one note at a time, but was added for flexibility.

PianoKey::~PianoKey

The class destructor relinquishes the storage for the key box and then invokes the base class to clean up the display list.

A Modified Keyboard

Now that the keyboard class is complete, it's time to add capability to record the sounds played. This addition entails a method for storing notes with chronological information so the melody plays back correctly. But how can we use the keyboard just described to do this? The choices here are only two:

1. Modify the class so it supports the new features directly.

2. Derive a new class from the basic keyboard class, and add the new features to it.

The basic rule in object-oriented programming is to reuse objects wherever possible, modifying them as needed. This reduces overall code size and complexity. Bugs will be easier to fix, too. Considering these advantages, this section creates the recording keyboard using the second choice.

A combination of classes implements the recording feature. The objects coordinate activities via shared variables. When you press a key, the new keyboard class sets a variable to the value of the pitch to be recorded. That's all you need to do. A separate object stores music events, an activity described in the next section.

The derived keyboard class is *Keyboard*. The following listings show the files needed. Note the missing class destructor. The base class has an adequate destructor function, so there is no need to replicate it. Little code is needed to make the new *Keyboard* class.

Listing 13.3. The header file for class Keyboard.

```
#ifndef KEYBOARDHPP
#define KEYBOARDHPP

#include <string.h>

#include "piano.hpp"
#include "events.hpp"

class Keyboard: public PianoKeyboard {

    int* current_frequency;

public:

    Keyboard(int, int, int*, int octave = 1);
    void KeyPressed(int frequency);
    void KeyReleased(int frequency);
};

#endif
```

Listing 13.4. The implementation of class Keyboard.

```
#include "keyboard.hpp"

Keyboard::Keyboard(int x, int y,
            int* event, int octave) :
            PianoKeyboard(x, y, octave)
{
    current_frequency = event;
}

void Keyboard::KeyPressed(int frequency)
{
    PianoKeyboard::KeyPressed(frequency);

    // log the key event
    *current_frequency = frequency;
}

void Keyboard::KeyReleased(int frequency)
{
```

```
PianoKeyboard::KeyReleased(frequency);

// log the key event
*current_frequency = 0;
}
```

Function Descriptions

Keyboard::Keyboard

The class constructor saves the reference to the shared variable set when you press or release a key. The function invokes the base class constructor to create the keyboard itself. The *octave* parameter defaults to the middle DO octave, if missing. Note that the usual *Display* function is missing in the derived class, because the ase-class function provides the features needed.

Keyboard::KeyPressed

This function first calls the base class's equivalent function to issue sound and then sets the shared variable to the pitch of the key pressed. Other objects can then handle the event.

Keyboard::KeyReleased

This function first calls the base class's equivalent function to silence the speaker and then sets the shared variable to zero so that other objects can handle the event.

The Melody Recorder

To record music, you must first decide what to record. One possibility is to store the levels of the square wave sent to the speaker, using a series of ones and zeros. A better way is to store musical *events*. This is the method most commonly used in digital music systems, and the one this application uses.

An event indicates that something has changed. The music keyboard can generate only two events: keystrokes and key releases. The recording object contains an array for saving these events. The most economical way is to tag each event with the time it occurred. Pressing a key and releasing it saves two events, no matter how long you hold the key down. This is a good technique, used also in MIDI systems, but it's too complicated for this simple application.

Instead this section uses the built-in *Update* animation function to do all the work. The top-level module invokes the *Update* function for all icons in the display list as often as possible. If the animated icons aren't numerous, this procedure results in smooth animation. For the recorder, this means that successive calls to *Update* are chronologically close together, giving good control over the duration of a note.

The technique is simple, but not without problems. The main drawback is that the time elapsed between two calls to *Update* depends not only on the number of icons in the display list, but also on the speed of your computer. For purposes of this discussion, it isn't a serious problem. When you record a melody, the frequency of *Update* calls is different from that during playback; thus the sounds played back have a slightly (but unnoticeably) different tempo from the original melody.

Something is still missing, though. How does the object know what to record? How does it know whether to record or playback? Using variables shared between the keyboard and the recorder provides a clean solution. Note that these variables are *shared*, but not global. They are local to whatever function controls the piano recorder page. The manipulation of these variables controls the actions of the recorder, which I will implement in the class *Melody*.

My simple recorder needs only three shared variables. The first one tells it the mode of operation (such as Stop, Record, and Rewind). The second indicates the tape count value. At the beginning of the melody its value is zero, and it increments as you record or play back a melody. The third tells it *what* to record from moment to moment, if anything. Listing 13.5. shows the files required by class *Melody*.

Listing 13.5. The header file for class Melody.

```
#ifndef MELODYHPP
#define MELODYHPP

#include "icon.hpp"
#include "events.hpp"
```

```
// establish the possible states of the recorder
enum RECORDING_STATE {
  STOP,
  REWIND,
  FAST_FORWARD,
  PLAY,
  RECORD
};

// over 2 minutes worth of music, on AT-286 machines
#define MAX_RECORDED_EVENTS 10000

class Melody: public Icon {

protected:
    int* recorder_mode;
    int* event_counter;
    int* current_note;
    int* event;
public:

    Melody(int* mode, int* counter, int* note);
    void Display() {}
    void Update();
    ~Melody();
};

#endif
```

Listing 13.6. The implementation of class Melody.

```
#include "melody.hpp"

Melody::Melody(int* mode, int* counter, int* note)
:
        Icon(-1, -1, -1, -1)
{
    // save references to state variables
    recorder_mode = mode;
    event_counter = counter;
    current_note = note;

    // set the tape counter to the beginning
    *event_counter = 0;

    // create the array for storing the melody
    event = new int [MAX_RECORDED_EVENTS];

    // clear out any garbage in the recorder
    for (int i = 0; i < MAX_RECORDED_EVENTS; i++)
```

Listing 13.6 Continues

Listing 13.6 Continued

```
            event [i] = 0;
    }

    void Melody::Update()
    {
        int frequency;
        static int last_frequency;

        switch (*recorder_mode) {
        case STOP:
          if (last_frequency == 0) return;
          EventsHandler->SoundOff();
          last_frequency = 0;
          return;
        case REWIND:
          EventsHandler->SoundOff();
          if (*event_counter >= 10)
            *event_counter -= 10;
          else if (*event_counter >= 1)
            *event_counter -= 1;
          return;
        case FAST_FORWARD:
          EventsHandler->SoundOff();
          if (*event_counter < MAX_RECORDED_EVENTS - 10)
            *event_counter += 10;
          else if (*event_counter <
    MAX_RECORDED_EVENTS - 1)
            *event_counter += 1;
          return;
        case RECORD:
          if (*event_counter <0) return;
          if (*event_counter >= MAX_RECORDED_EVENTS)
    return;
          event [*event_counter] = *current_note;
          (*event_counter)++;
          return;
        case PLAY:
          if (*event_counter < 0) *event_counter = 0;
          if (*event_counter > MAX_RECORDED_EVENTS)
            *event_counter = 0;

          // make a short sound
          frequency = event [*event_counter];
          (*event_counter)++;
          if (frequency == last_frequency) return;
          last_frequency = frequency;
          if (frequency)
            EventsHandler->SoundOn(frequency);
          else
            EventsHandler->SoundOff();
```

```
          return;
     }
}

Melody::~Melody()
{
     delete event;
}
```

Function Descriptions

Melody::Melody

The class constructor saves the pointers to the shared variables that will control the operation of the sound recorder. Class *Melody* writes into the variable *event_counter,* which then controls the number displayed on the *TapeCounter* object described in the next section. An array is dynamically allocated to store melodies. The array is subsequently used to store notes in the form of integer frequencies.

Melody::Update

This function actually runs the recorder. The shared variable *recorder_mode governs the behavior of class *Melody*. During the recording mode, *Melody::Update()* stores the value of the note currently being played in the array *events*. This is done by sampling the variable *current_note at a constant rate, with each sample being stored sequentially in the array. During playback, the process is inverted: the array *event* is sequentially read, and any notes stored are emitted as sound. The interval between successive calls to *Melody::Update()* defines the basic sampling rate of this simple digital-recording system. To obtain good results, the execution time of *Update()::Melody* should be about the same in both the recording and playback modes.

Melody::~Melody

The class destructor de-allocates the storage array for the melody and then calls the base class destructor to remove the object from the display list.

The Tape Counter

This icon shows how far you are in a recorded sequence. When a *Melody* object is first created, the tape counter object shows the value zero, because no tune has been recorded yet. During the recording phase, the tape counter advances slowly, emulating the way a real tape would behave. Pressing the Fast Forward or Rewind buttons causes the tape counter value to change rapidly. Class *TapeCounter* uses the shared variable *tape_count as the value to display. This variable is manipulated by the recorder control object, shown later. Figure 13.2 shows a *TapeCounter* object, and listings 13.7 and 13.8 show the code for class *TapeCounter*.

Fig. 13.2. An object of class TapeCounter.

Listing 13.7. The header file for class TapeCounter.

```
#ifndef COUNTERHPP
#define COUNTERHPP

#include <stdio.h>

#include "icon.hpp"
#include "box.hpp"
#include "graphics.hpp"
#include "events.hpp"
#include "legend.hpp"

#define TAPE_COUNTER_WIDTH 95
#define TAPE_COUNTER_HEIGHT 44
#define TAPE_COUNTER_LEGEND_HEIGHT 14

class TapeCounter: public Icon {

protected:

    ShadedBox* box;
    int *tape_count;
    int last_count;

public:

    TapeCounter(int, int, int*);
```

```
        void Display();
        void Update();
        virtual ~TapeCounter();
};

#endif
```

Listing 13.8. The implementation of class TapeCounter.

```
#include "counter.hpp"

TapeCounter::TapeCounter(int x, int y, int* count)
:
    Icon(x, y, x + TAPE_COUNTER_WIDTH,
                y + TAPE_COUNTER_HEIGHT)
{
    // capture the reference to the count value
    tape_count = count;

    // set to a negative value in order to
    // force Update() to shown the initial count
    last_count = -1;

    // create the tape counter box
    box = new ShadedBox(x1, y1,
                x2 - x1, y2 - y1,
                BLACK,
                BRIGHT_RED,
                GRAY);
}

void TapeCounter::Display()
{
    // show the backdop box
    box->Display();

    // partition off the legend area
    BOX_TYPE area;
    area.x1 = x1 + 2;
    area.y1 = y1 + TAPE_COUNTER_LEGEND_HEIGHT + 2;
    area.x2 = x2 - 2;
    area.y2 = area.y1;
    GraphicsHandler->DrawLine(BRIGHT_RED,
                    SOLID_LINE,
                    &area);

    // display the name of the icon
    Legend value;
    area.y1 = y1;
    value.Center(&area, BRIGHT_RED, "Tape Count");
```

Listing 13.8 Continues

229

Listing 13.8 Continued

```
    }

    void TapeCounter::Update()
    {
        // abort unless the tape count has changed
        if (*tape_count == last_count) return;

        // store value of this tape count
        last_count = *tape_count;

        // erase the previous count
        BOX_TYPE box;
        box.x1 = x1 + 3;
        box.y1 = y1 + TAPE_COUNTER_LEGEND_HEIGHT + 3;
        box.x2 = x2 - 3;
        box.y2 = y2 - 3;
        GraphicsHandler->FillBox(GRAY, &box);

        // display the current count value
        Legend value;
        char string [20];
        sprintf(string, "%d", *tape_count);
        value.Center(&box, BRIGHT_RED, string);
    }

    TapeCounter::~TapeCounter()
    {
        delete box;
    }
```

Function Descriptions

TapeCounter::TapeCounter

The class constructor saves the reference to the shared control variable and then creates a shaded box for itself. The constructor function does not update the display.

TapeCounter::Display

This function displays a shaded box and partitions off the lower portion so it has room for the icon's legend. This function does not show the actual value of the tape counter, because this is considered to be the domain of the *Update* animation function.

TapeCounter::Update

This function is called continuously by the top level and provides the animation effect for the tape counter. It checks the current value of the count to see whether it has already been displayed. If not, the function shows a new value.

TapeCounter::~TapeCounter

This destructor de-allocates the storage used by the icon's shaded box and invokes the base class to remove itself from the display list.

The Recorder Controls

To use the digital recorder designed, there must be a way to control it. Any cassette player has controls labeled Play, Record, Rewind, etc. to handle tape motion. These controls can be issued only one at a time. For example, it is wrong to press the Play and Rewind buttons at the same time. To implement such a control as a class is trivial, because a *HorizontalSelector* object performs exactly the operations needed. It shows a series of buttons laid out side-by-side, and allows only one button to be active at a given time. Class *Melody* requires a total of five buttons to control it, resulting in a control similar to the one shown in figure 13.3.

The following code fragment will create such an icon:

```
static int recorder_mode;
HorizontalSelector* tape_controls =
    new HorizontalSelector(100, 300,
            "Recorder Controls",
            &recorder_mode,
            0,
            "Stop",
            "Rewind",
            "Forward",
            "Play",
            "Record");
```

The control variable `recorder_mode` is declared static just in case the function creating the object exits before the icon is deleted. The '0' parameter indicates that there is no activation function for the control. The only side effect of clicking on it is the change of value for the shared variable `recorder_mode`.

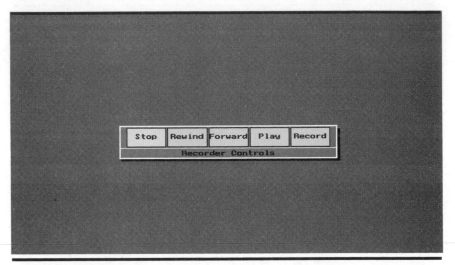

Fig. 13.3. The tape recorder control selector.

The PianoPage Class

Because the basic control surface is organized by pages, this section puts all the controls for the piano recorder in a special page class called *PianoPage*. Not only does this make all the objects appear in the same file, but it takes advantage of the *Page* class features to do much of the work. The mechanics for deriving a page are always the same. Listings 13.9 and 13.10 show the header and implementation files for class *PianoPage*.

Listing 13.9. The header file for class PianoPage.

```
#ifndef PIANOPAGEHPP
#define PIANOPAGEHPP

#include "page.hpp"
#include "database.hpp"
#include "selector.hpp"
#include "keyboard.hpp"
#include "melody.hpp"
#include "counter.hpp"

class PianoPage: public Page {

    COLOR_TYPE title_color;
```

```
        static int recorder_mode;
        static int keyboard_note;
        static int counter;

        HorizontalSelector* tape_controls;
        Keyboard* keyboard_one;
        Keyboard* keyboard_two;
        Melody* melody_recorder;
        TapeCounter* tape_counter;

public:

        PianoPage();
        void Display();
        virtual ~PianoPage();
};

extern void OpenPianoPage();

#endif
```

Listing 13.10. The implementation of class PianoPage.

```
#include "pianopg.hpp"

PianoPage::PianoPage() : Page("A Piano Recorder")
{
        tape_controls = new HorizontalSelector(100, 250,
                        "Recorder Controls",
                        &recorder_mode,
                        0,
                        "Stop",
                        "Rewind",
                        "Forward",
                        "Play",
                        "Record");

        keyboard_one = new Keyboard(5, 25, &
                        keyboard_note);
        int x = 5 + KEYBOARD_WIDTH;
        keyboard_two = new Keyboard(x, 25,
                        &keyboard_note, 2);

        melody_recorder = new Melody(&recorder_mode,
                        &counter,
                        &keyboard_note);
        tape_counter = new TapeCounter(450, 250, &counter);
}
```

Listing 13.10 Continues

Listing 13.10 Continued

```
void PianoPage::Display()
{
      Page::Display();

      tape_controls->Display();
      keyboard_one->Display();
      keyboard_two->Display();
      tape_counter->Display();
}

PianoPage::~PianoPage()
{
      // destroy all objects on the screen
      delete tape_controls;
      delete keyboard_one;
      delete keyboard_two;
      delete melody_recorder;
      delete tape_counter;
}

void OpenPianoPage()
{
      // get next page ready
      PianoPage* new_page = new PianoPage();

      // create new page
      CurrentScreen->NewWorkArea(new_page);
      CurrentScreen->DisplayWorkArea();
}
```

The Complete Program

Now that all the icons have been created and organized onto a page, it's easy to put everything together into a working system. The last step remaining is to add the *PianoPage* into the rest of the GUI. You accomplish this task by inserting a reference to *PianoPage* into the page selector so that the page can be activated. This procedure involves modifying the global array *Pages* in the file *database.cpp*. This file contains the definition of all the global items, including one that specifies the page-selector actions. The complete listing for *database.cpp* is on the companion disk. Anytime you add an application-specific button to the page selector, you need to edit the global array *Pages*. The following listing shows the *Pages* array for a system with only the *PianoPage* item.

Listing 13.11. The Pages *array with one item.*

```
extern void OpenPianoPage();
PAGE_BUTTON_DEFINITION Pages [MAX_PAGE_BUTTON] = {
  "Piano",      OpenPianoPage,
   0,            0,
};
```

In array *Page* the first field is the legend that appears on a page-selector button, and the second is the function invoked when you click the button with the mouse. Notice how the array ends with a null pointer in the page-legend field.

A Path of Destruction

The various objects used in building the keyboard recorder are simple. The program's power comes from putting together lots of objects. It's easy to forget how many objects get created and how the class hierarchy governs them, because C++ often hides the details. To illustrate how much activity goes on behind the scenes, the next paragraph traces the sequence of events when the recorder page is removed from the screen by issuing the statement

```
delete page;
```

where 'page' was an object of class *PianoPage*. Listing 13.12 shows the destructor calls. Note that virtual destructors handle many of the destruction details.

Listing 13.12. The destruction of a PianoPage *object.*

```
PianoPage::~PianoPage();
    delete tap_controls;
        Selector::~Selector();
            delete selector box;
                ShadedBox::~ShadedBox();
                    delete bottom_box;
                        Icon::~Icon();
                    delete top_box;
                        Icon::~Icon();
                    Icon::~Icon();
            delete each button
                Button::~Button();
                    delete box;
                        Icon::~Icon();
```

Listing 13.12 Continues

Listing 13.12 Continued

```
                              Icon::~Icon();
          delete keyboard_one;
              PianoKeyboard::~PianoKeyboard();
                  delete each note
                      PianoKey::~PianoKey();
                          delete key;
                              Icon::~Icon();
                          Icon::~Icon();
          delete keyboard_two;
              PianoKeyboard::~PianoKeyboard();
                  delete each note
                      PianoKey::~PianoKey();
                          delete key;
                              Icon::~Icon();
                          Icon::~Icon();
          delete melody_recorder;
              Melody::~Melody();
                  delete event;
                      Icon::~Icon();
          delete tape_counter;
              TapeCounter::~TapeCounter();
                  delete box;
                      ShadedBox::~ShadedBox();
                          delete bottom_box;
                              Icon::~Icon();
                          delete top_box;
                              Icon::~Icon();
                      Icon::~Icon();

      Page::~Page();
          delete title;
              Description::~Description();
                  delete box;
                      Icon::~Icon();
                  Icon::~Icon();
          Icon::~Icon();
```

14

Machine Dependencies and Insulation Techniques

This book uses the term *insulation* to indicate a separation between the code in an application and the specifics of the machine it runs on. Insulating from these dependencies gives rise to *portability*. Because this book is about C++ in general, and Turbo C++ in particular, you'll wonder why I address the issue at all.

First of all, there is no such thing as a standard PC configuration. There are tens of millions of PCs in the world, and probably just as many different combinations of motherboards, display adaptors, modem cards, mice, memory boards, hard disks, and so on. If you want to write a single program that runs on several different machine configurations, you have to maintain a degree of insulation from the machine.

As it turns out, writing portable code is important for another reason, less obvious perhaps. The outstanding quality of the Turbo C++ implementation makes debugging code extremely fast on a PC; it is a good test vehicle for code not designed to run on a PC at all. Most programmers of embedded systems rely heavily on simulators and emulators to get their code running on a target machine. Their development cycle is straightforward, albeit slow: edit, cross-compile, link, transfer, emulate. To complete a single iteration of the cycle may easily take more than an hour. Finding a bug with an emulator often entails working at the assembly language level, so most of the power and advantages of C++ are lost at this stage.

If you properly insulate your code from target machine dependencies, you can develop the code on the PC, test it interactively, and debug it—without ever leaving the Turbo C++ Integrated Development Environment. You reduce the typical edit-compile-link-test-debug cycle from hours to minutes. A good question at this point: "How does code run on a PC when it was designed and written to run on a different processor with a different operating system, or even without one?" The answer: "By designing it carefully and knowing what to look out for."

First you need to identify which parts of a system are invariant across hardware implementations and which are not. The following is a list of things often (or always) machine dependent.

- Display adaptors

- Screen resolution

- Screen colors available

- Mouse programming

- Memory size and architecture

- I/O

- File structures

- Byte ordering for integers

- Floating point encoding

- Use of interrupts

- Operating system calls

- Graphics functions

- Execution speed

- Directory structures

The list includes just *some* of the things from which you should insulate the application. It seems like an overwhelming task, but if faced early on in the development cycle, it is simpler to handle. However, that code can be portable to **any** machine is practically a utopia, both because of the infinite variations in machines and the features of C (C++) not completely portable across implementations. Compilers designed for Unix will make certain assumptions about the environment not necessarily correct for a DOS system. With UNIX multitasking at work, programs can run differently than under DOS. Moreover, embedded systems often have no operating system at all and make intensive use of interrupts.

In the following sections, I'll examine some areas of programming that should get special emphasis in machine-dependency insulation.

Computer Displays

When writing applications for PCs, you never know what kind of display the user will have, so you have two choices:

1. You can make the program run with a single specific display adaptor, such as EGA. When you start the program, it goes out and checks the type of adaptor installed. If it finds the correct one, the program runs; otherwise a message is printed and the program terminates.

2. You can design the system to run on a range of different adaptors, with the program detecting the configuration at startup time.

The second solution allows more flexibility, but it is obviously more complicated. The first thing to design is a virtual screen layout, with a resolution adequate for high resolution output, such as 4000 x 3000 pixels. This offers a theoretical resolution as good as 35 mm film, thus representing a superset of the characteristics of PC display adaptors. Working within the framework of the virtual screen, your application deals with graphics using the virtual coordinates. A *Graphics* object manages the screen, such as the one introduced in this book, which will perform dynamic conversion of the virtual coordinates into whatever graphics system is supported by the display adaptor detected by the program.

The same insulation would also be provided for the screen colors. Given the variety of palette and color arrangements available on different systems, the application program should adopt a virtual color scheme, such as the one used in Microsoft Windows. The color of each pixel is defined by its red, green, and blue saturation. Using 8 bits for each color, you obtain 256 x 256 x 256 variations adequate for even the most demanding artistic renditions. The *Graphics* object would then perform the conversion of the virtual colors into physical ones, utilizing the capabilities of the display adaptor detected. This conversion may make use of pattern filling, to simulate colors not available directly, or convert unsupported colors into predefined ones. It also supports the conversion of virtual colors into shades of gray for monochrome systems.

With the virtual screen in place, you next need a complete set of core functions to support graphics, utilizing standard C features. Unfortunately this is not possible. The C++ language, just as ANSI C, makes no attempts to standardize or even define graphics functions. Experts have given enormous attention to standardizing device I/O, with files and streams, but they have overlooked the vital graphics output. Perhaps in coming years with the advent of low-cost megapixel systems we'll see more attention given to developing a standard library of portable graphics functions.

Hardware Dependencies

It is hard to find two PCs configured exactly the same. Different classes of personal computers even use a different processor altogether. Writing a program insensitive of hardware is extremely challenging. Hardware dependencies crop up all over, ranging from programming styles to execution speed to event handling. The following sections deal with a few of the salient hardware problems.

Use of Assembly Language

One of the most pervasive degenerations in high-performance systems is the use of inline assembly language. This may make the code faster, but it is a nightmare for portability. There are several ways to incorporate assembly language into a program, some better than others. The worst is inline code. Spreading assembly language all over a system makes it very difficult to keep track of it. A better way is to identify all the low-level hardware functions and to relegate them to a single module. Many of these functions are in assembly language. To port the project to a different machine would ideally require modifying only the hardware interface module. In practice things are never this easy. Hardware dependencies are usually not solved by merely avoiding assembly language.

Programming Hardware Devices

Programs always need hardware to run. Operating systems provide some insulation from some hardware operations, such as disk handling and character-level writing on the user display. Often you need to access other hardware or gain tighter control of it. The only choice you have is to program the devices yourself. Although this choice inevitably results in non-portable code, there are methods which lend themselves to porting.

A possible C++ solution is to create a *Hardware* class that hides all aspects of hardware programming and handling. Consider a typical PC architecture with some of the devices you wish to control directly: the timer chip, the display adaptor, and the serial communications adaptor. The *Hardware* class embodies three subclasses *Timer*, *Graphics*, and *CommPort*. Vectoring through the *Hardware* class interface, you can read and write to various chip registers and invoke higher level hardware functions. The *CommPort* class could have functions like *SendCharacter* and *ReadCharacter* or even allow installable interrupt service routines.

You can write most functions dealing with hardware in C++ directly, resorting to assembly language only in extreme cases and only at the lowest level possible.

Byte Ordering and Word Length

An insidious problem for portable programs is the byte ordering scheme used by the CPU. The Motorola family of 68000 processors uses a notation referred to as *positive sex*. These machines address memory in bytes. A 32-bit integer occupies 4 bytes. The most significant byte is at the lowest address, the least significant one at the highest address. Intel processors have *negative sex*. The lowest address of a 32-bit integer is occupied by the least significant byte, so all the bytes are in reverse order.

A program should never rely on byte ordering used by integers, or the format used in storing floating point numbers, or the word length of a machine. The following code fragment would execute correctly on a machine with positive sex, but not on others.

Listing 14.1. A sample code fragment that relies on a special byte ordering scheme to work.

```
/* output a 16-bit value on an 8-bit port */
union {
  int word;
  char byte [2];
} variable;

/* get the 16-bit integer */
variable.word = integer;

/* send the most significant byte */
SendByte(variable. byte [0]);

/* send the least significant byte */
SendByte(variable. byte [1]);
```

The next listing shows code that performs the same task, but results in portable code.

Listing 14.2. A portable implementation that divides an integer into 2 bytes.

```
/* use an explicit variable */
unsigned char byte;

/* get the more significant byte */
/* (which isn't necessarily the MOST */
/* significant). */
byte = (integer >> 8) & 0xFF;
SendByte(byte);

/* get the least significant byte */
byte = integer & 0xFF;
SendByte(byte);
```

Note that both listings take a value, stored in an integer, and split it into two 8-bit parts. This is a machine-dependent operation, because integers can occupy more or less than 16 bits. Never assume that integers are 16 or 32 bits in length. Machines define the size of integers, longs, chars and floats as best suited for their architectre. I've seen integers ranging from 8 to 64 bits in size.

Operating System Dependencies

Most GUIs are designed to run under an operating system (OS). This is normally an advantage, because all the complexities of disk I/O, file management, and system housekeeping are handled automatically. ANSI C and C++ have a good I/O library as far as streams are concerned, so most stream operations are portable if performed correctly. Unfortunately many other system resources are totally ignored by standards. Making use of them clearly results in nonportable code. Among these are the following:

1. Timer functions allowing programmable resolution. In many situations you need to track time in increments too fine for the OS to handle. Example: you must invoke a function after 3550 microseconds, and you don't want to use a *Wait* function because you need to keep the system alive for the delay period. With a programmable timer arrangement, you need the OS to invoke the function as an interrupt-service routine after the designated delay.

2. Mouse hardware. There are no standards for dealing with mice or more generic pointing devices across operating systems. This situation suggests the arrangement shown in Chapter 1, in which a *Mouse* class was implemented to protect the GUI from mouse details.

3. Graphics hardware. Another area of **huge** problems. Not only has C/C++ failed to deal with graphics issues, but so have operating systems. Luckily the situation doesn't appear completely hopeless. With the emerging popularity of high-powered graphics processors designed around the Motorola 88000 and Texas Instruments 34020 processors, graphics command languages may be on their way to a consensus, which could bring about some degree of standardization.

4. Audio hardware. Most computers ignore sound generation altogether. The most you can get in some cases is a *beep*. If you deal with audio output in a system, the best method is to create a *Sound* class that insulates the hardware completely. This would possibly utilize a virtual sound system, defining frequency, volume, stereo parameters, attack-sustain-delay envelopes, timbre, etc. in machine-independent terms. The class would then map the virtual sound into the best sound reproducible on a specific machine. PC class machines have crude sound capability, but other systems use multi-voice synthesizer hardware or even stereo digital audio processors.

5. Keyboard problems. All C/C++ compilers provide standard functions for reading from standard input, usually the system keyboard. They treat the device like a stream, but this doesn't always work satisfactorily. The first problem is that the ASCII

or extended ASCII set is insufficient for handling all keys: shift keys, ALT keys, CAPS LOCK, arrow keys, and function keys are only some of the codes missing from the set. A well-designed keyboard handler would ideally have mapping table, converting the machine-dependent key values into a suitable machine-independent format.

Another problem is detecting keyboard activity. Often you need only to check whether a key is pressed, without reading the key itself. With Turbo C++ you can use the *kbhit()* or *bioskey()* functions, but these are not portable. With standard I/O functions you could use *getch()* and *ungetch()*, but it seems to be a kluge, is inefficient, and doesn't work in some cases. What if your application is checking the status of the SHIFT or ALT key ? For example version 2.0 of Turbo C displayed a new help line at the bottom of the screen if you held the ALT key down for a few seconds.

And what about the auto-repeat rate of the keyboard? When you press a key down on the PC, the key is sent immediately to the system. If you hold the key down, it is sent repeatedly after a short delay. Some systems need to take control over this process, to defeat it, to accelerate it, or modify it in some other way. A special class should be instituted to deal with the keyboard, insulating all these variations from the GUI.

Critical Errors

During the execution of a program, many things beyond the control of a GUI can go wrong. Often these depend on hardware failures or runtime errors that prevent the program from continuing execution. These failures are often referred to as *critical errors*. The following is a list of some of them.

- Printer errors

    Printer not ready

    Paper out

    General failure

- File errors

    File doesn't exist

    Read-only files

    Locked files

- Disk errors

    Directory full

    Disk full

    Disk write protected

    Drive not ready

- Math errors

    Divide by zero

    Domain error

    Value out of range

You should deal with all of them so the system has the chance to recover gracefully. Users don't expect or appreciate messages like

Messages like these immediately give the impression of an unfinished product. Just as bad, if not worse, are errors that abruptly terminate a program, such as a stack overflow or math error. Graceful recovery is the process through which a program notifies the operator of a problem, allowing options for continuing execution. Never should you lose control of the screen or the program to the OS.

With DOS, interrupt 0x24 handles hardware errors. Turbo C++ uses the function *harderr()* to install a user handler. Hardware errors vectored through this handler are the following:

- Disk errors

- Drive errors

- Printer errors

- General failures

Consult the *Turbo C++ Reference Manual*'s *harderr()* function for more details on these errors.

DOS deals with math errors in two different ways. When you attempt floating point operations with invalid arguments, a special *signal* mechanism traps errors. These can be considered low-level math errors, occurring during arithmetic operations such as multiplication and division. Examples of such errors are:

- Numeric overflow

- Numeric underflow

- Division by zero

In order to process these errors, the GUI must install proper handlers using the *signal()* function. Consult the *Turbo C++ Reference Manual* for more details.

The other category of math errors is generated in transcendental functions, such as *exp()* or *arctan()*. You can consider these to be high-level errors; the compiler-dependent math library, not DOS, traps them. With Turbo C++ you install a handler with the function *matherr())*. Errors processed by this handler are the following:

- Domain errors

- Overflow errors

- Underflow errors

Consult the *Turbo C++ Reference Manual* for more details.

Asynchronous Events

During the execution of a program, the user can force a special event under DOS, which should always be handled explicitly: typing Control-Break on the keyboard. When this happens, DOS traps the event and invokes a handler through interrupt 0x23. The default error-recovery sequence is to terminate the user program and return to DOS. A better use for the event is to have it interrupt lengthy operations in progress and return to the GUI top-level module. If you initiated a long compilation and then decided to abort it, the Control-Break sequence would allow you to halt the compilation without exiting all the way to DOS.

Conclusion

Machine independent code is not easy to achieve. The most significant ingredient required is experience, both with C/C++ and general-purpose computers. The first time you really HAVE to port a project to another machine, you discover how important good design practices are. Anytime you have the luxury of dealing with standardized features of hardware or programming languages, everything is simpler. But standard features are hard to come by.

The greatest problem in standardizing is *people*. Everyone has different needs and different perceptions of what an ideal computer should be. Graphics, audio, operating systems, etc., will probably fail to converge on truly universal standards for all machines. More likely, the methods used by each of the major computer camps will be refined following parallel paths.

GUIs are being developed for all types of computers, from PCs to supercomputers. All are related to the same system first built at Xerox PARC in the '70s. They all share basic features of intuitiveness, use of graphics, and pointing devices, but they do not standardize many other features.

Users don't really care *why* systems are different: they are not involved in corporate marketing strategies and profit-loss statements. Their concern is for computers that are easier to use and understand. Perhaps GUIs will converge on common ideas, so a person familiar with *one* computer will be able to use *any* computer.

Inevitably, the days of obscure OS-command line prompts are numbered.

Object Reference Guide

This section contains a list of the salient objects used throughout the book. The companion disk contains the source code for all of them. The classes are listed in alphabetical order, but class names don't always coincide with the files they are saved in. Not all classes have constructors or destructors, especially if they are derived. Some files that contain multiple classes can be referenced more than once.

Class: *Box*

Description: This class and its derived ones define rectangular boxes displayed on the screen. Boxes have selectable shade, border, and inside colors. For simplicity, only solid colors are used for area filling. Boxes are the normal support objects for most displayable items and are seldom used by themselves.

Parent class: *Icon*

Child classes: None

Member functions: Constructor, Color, Display

Files used: box.hpp and box.cpp

Class: *Clock*

Description: This class implements a digital clock sensitive to world time zones. It uses animation features to run itself autonomously, and multiple clocks can be run together on different time zones.

Parent class: *Icon*

Child classes: *ShadedBox*

Member functions: constructor, Display , Update, destructor

Files used: clock.hpp and clock.cpp

Class: *ClockPage*

Description: This page is available in the demo program by selecting page *Clocks*. It shows an example of multiple digital clocks running on different time zones, underscoring the unobtrusive nature of animated objects.

Parent class: *Page*

Child classes: *Clock*

Member functions: constructor, destructor

Files used: clocks.hpp and clocks.cpp

Class: *Configuration*

Description: Objects of this class allow a system to load a previous configuration stored on disk automatically . When none are available, all variables are set to their default values. The class saves the values for all variables when the application program terminates.

Parent class: None

Child classes: None

Member functions: constructor, UseConfigurationFile, UseDefaults, destructor

Files used: config.hpp and config.cpp

Class: *Delay*

Description: This class implements a self-calibrating delay object that adjusts itself to the speed of the machine it runs on. It is useful especially for delays in the millisecond range when the standard *sleep* function cannot be used.

Parent class: None

Child classes: None

Member functions: constructor, DelayOneMillisecond, DosTickCount, Wait

Files used: delay.hpp and delay.cpp

See also: *Mouse*

Class: *Description*

Description: This class creates a box and allows a string to be displayed inside it. It is handy for title areas and legends.

Parent class: *Icon*

Child classes: *Box*

Member functions: constructor, SetText, Display, destructor

Files used: descrip.hpp and descrip.cpp

See also: *Legend*

Class: *Die*

Description: This class implements the computer die, visible on the *Games* page of the demo program. Clicking it makes it "roll" and issue a characteristic sound.

Parent class: *MonostablePushButton*

Child classes: *RandomNumber*

Member functions: constructor, MakeSound, GetNextRoll, Update

Files used: die.hpp and die.cpp

Class: *Events*

Description: This is the main event handler for the GUI. It insulates most of the machine dependencies of the system from the application, handling the mouse, the timer chip, and the keyboard.

Parent class: None

Child classes: *Mouse*, *Delay*

Member functions: constructor, ShowMouseCursor, HideMouseCursor, ProcessMouseActions, GetKeyPressed, AnyKeysPressed, ProcessUserKeys, SystemTime, CurrentTime, Wait, Beep, SoundOn, SoundOff, DisableInterrupts, EnableInterrupts

Files used: events.hpp and events.cpp

Class: *GamePage*

Description: This class defines the *Games* page available in the demo program.

Parent class: *Page*

Child classes: *ToneButton*, *Die*, *Lotto*

Member functions: constructor, Display, destructor

Files used: games.hpp and games.cpp

Class: *Graphics*

Description: This class provides support for graphics drawing functions. Both EGA and VGA adaptors are supported, using 640 x 350 resolution. Sixteen colors are available, but color palettes are not used. There are two versions of the class, one for TurboC++ and one for Zortech C++. The macros **BORLAND** and **ZORTECH** in file *constant.hpp* will indicate which version to use.

Parent class: None

Child classes: None

Member functions: constructor, DrawDot, DrawBox, DrawCircle, DrawLine, FillBox, FillCircle, PutString, FontWidth, FontHeight, ScreenWidth, ScreenHeight, Terminate, destructor

Files used: bgraphics.hpp (Borland version) and bgraphics.cpp zgraphics.hpp (Zortech version) and zgraphics.cpp

---

Class: *Icon*

Description: This is the root class for all objects that can be displayed. It provides display-list handling for screen support.

Parent class: None

Child classes: None

Member functions: constructor, Display, Update, LeftButtonPressed, LeftButtonReleased, LeftButtonDragged, KeyTyped, destructor

Files used: icon.hpp and icon.cpp

See also: *Screen*

Class: *Keyboard*

Description: This class defines the keyboard object used for recording and may be seen in page *Piano* of the demo program.

Parent class: *PianoKeyboard*

Child classes: None

Member functions: constructor, KeyPressed, KeyReleased

Files used: keyboard.hpp and keyboard.cpp

See also: *Piano*

Class: *Legend*

Description: This class takes a string and displays it inside a rectangular area on the screen. The formatting instructions available are left-aligned, centered, and right-aligned, and only the string is displayed not any backdrop boxes or backgrounds.

Parent class: None

Child classes: None

Member functions: Left, Center, Right

Files used: legend.hpp and legend.cpp

See also: class *Description*

Class: *DisplayList*

Description: This class supports the linked list used to store all the objects shown on the screen. The list facilitates mouse and keyboard processing by keeping its objects in chronological order.

Parent class: None

Child classes: *DisplayListNode*

Member functions: constructor, DeleteCurrentNode, FatalListError, Size, AddItem, RemoveItem, CurrentItem, NextItem, GotoBeginning, GotoEnd, destructor

Files used: listmgr.hpp and listmgr.cpp

See also: *Screen, Icon*

Class: *Lotto*

Description: This class defines an object that randomly chooses 6 numbers in the range 1..49. It can be seen on page *Games* of the demo program. Class *Lotto* illustrates some of the techniques for deriving classes.

Parent class: *HorizontalSelector*

Child classes: *RandomNumber*

Member functions: constructor, Refresh, Clear, MakeSound, NextPick, Update, LeftButtonPressed, LeftButtonReleased

Files used: lotto.hpp and lotto.cpp

Class: *Melody*

Description: This class is one of the few not designed to be displayed. It works in conjunction with other classes to record music. To work, it needs there to be a source of sound and an object to control the recorder.

Parent class: *Icon*

Child classes: None

Member functions: constructor, Update, destructor

Files used: melody.hpp and melody.cpp

Class: *Mouse*

Description: This class provides an interface to a Microsoft compatible mouse driver. It fully insulates the application from the driver and uses a coordinate system that coincides with the one used by the screen.

Parent class: None

Child classes: None

Member functions: constructor, RightHandedCartesian, ButtonInfo, MouseCommand, Show, Hide, Status, SetPosition, ButtonPressed, ButtonReleased, SetXRange, SetYRange, LeftButtonDown, RightButtonDown, BothButtonsDown, destructor

Files used: mouse.hpp and mouse.cpp

See also: *Events*

Class: *Page*

Description: This class constitutes the base class for all application pages. It handles the title area and provides linkage to the display list. Because of the class constructor and destructor, most application pages need never deal with the display list details.

Parent class: *Icon*

Child classes: *Description*

Member functions: constructor, destructor

Files used: page.hpp and page.cpp

Class: *PageSelector*

Description: This class allows the selection of an application page, which is then displayed in the work area of the screen.

Parent class: *Icon*

Child classes: *PageButton*

Member functions: constructor, Display, Select, destructor

Files used: pagesel.hpp and pagesel.cpp

Class: *PianoKeyboard*

Description: This class implements a simple piano keyboard. It provides the base class for the recording keyboard shown on page *Piano* of the demo program.

Parent class: *Icon*

Child classes: *PianoKey*

Member functions: constructor, CreateWhiteKeys, CreateBlackKeys, Display, KeyPressed, KeyReleased, destructor

Files used: piano.hpp and piano.cpp

See also: *Keyboard*

Class: *PianoPage*

Description: This implements the entire *Piano* page shown in the demo program. It demonstrates the simplicity of deriving application pages.

Parent class: *Page*

Child classes: *HorizontalSelector*, *Keyboard*, *Melody*, *TapeCounter*

Member functions: constructor, Display, destructor

Files used: pianopg.hpp and pianopg.cpp

Class: *PingPong*

Description: This is the simplest animated class described in the book. *PingPong* objects are small rectangular figures that bounce around inside the work area of the screen.

Parent class: *Icon*

Child classes: None

Member functions: constructor, Paint, Erase, Display, Update, destructor

Files used: pingpong.hpp and pingpong.cpp

Class: *PingPongPage*

Description: This class defines a page with three ping-pong balls that bounce around in the work area. It demonstrates some of the principles of object animation. To see an example of a *PingPongPage* object, run the demo program and select page *PingPong*.

Child classes: *PingPong*

Member functions: constructor, destructor

Files used: ball.hpp and ball.cpp

Class: *PopupWindow*

Description: This is the base object for deriving application popup objects. It handles all the details of opening and closing windows, including the restoration of any background objects covered.

Parent class: *Icon*

Child classes: *ShadedBox, PopupWindowExitButton*

Member functions: constructor, Display, destructor

Files used: popup.hpp and popup.cpp

See also: *PopupWindowButton* and *PopupWindowExitButton*

Class: *PopupWindowButton*

Description: This is the class that drives the rest of the popup objects. It implements a button that makes a popup window appear when it is pressed, covering temporarily an area of the screen.

Parent class: *Icon*

Child classes: *ShadedBox, PopupWindow*

Member functions: constructor, Display, WindowOpened, Highlight, UnHighlight, LeftButttonPressed, LeftButtonReleased, destructor

Files used: popup.hpp and popup.cpp

See also: *PopupWindow* and *PopupWindowExitButton*

Class: *Pot*

Description: This is the base class for all potentiometers, vertical and horizontal. It manages the cursor, the setting, and other details.

Parent class: *Icon*

Child classes: *ShadedBox, Cursor*

Member functions: constructor, Display, Setting, SettingDisplay, destructor

Files used: pot.hpp and pot.cpp

Class: *PushButton*

Description: This is the base class for all types of pushbuttons. It displays a rectangular control, whose behavior may be overriden by derived classes.

Parent class: *Icon*

Child classes: *ShadedBox*

Member functions: constructor, CurrentState, SetLegend, Update, LeftButtonPressed, LeftButtonReleased, Display, Activate, destructor

Files used: pushbut.hpp and pushbut.cpp

Class: *RandomNumber*

Description: This class provides automatic randomization when an object is created. It allows random numbers to be treated with simplicity.

Parent class: *Icon*

Child classes: None

Member functions: constructor, NextValue

Files used: random.hpp and random.cpp

Class: *RecorderPage*

Description: This class implements the application page called *Recorder*, used in the demo program.

Parent class: *Page*

Child classes: *HorizontalSelector*, *AttenuatorPot*, *PopupWindowButton*

Member functions: constructor, Display, destructor

Files used: recorder.hpp and recorder.cpp

Class: *Screen*

Description: This class manages all the screen activity via the display list. It works with the *Events* class to dispatch mouse and keyboard events. It is one of the central classes for the entire GUI.

Parent class: None

Child classes: *DisplayList, Icon, PageSelector*

Member functions: constructor, NumberOfIcons, DisplayTemplate, ClearArea, ClearWorkArea, NewWorkArea, DisplayWorkArea, ReDraw, AddItem, RemoveItem, Update, LeftButtonChanged, CurrentIcon, LeftButtonDragged, KeyTyped, SetPageSelector, GetPageSelector, destructor

Files used: screen.hpp and screen.cpp

See also: *Events, Mouse, DisplayList*

Class: *Selector*

Description: This is the base class for horizontal and vertical selectors. It handles the details of display list interfacing and child button selecting.

Parent class: *Icon*

Child classes: *ShadedBox, Button*

Member functions: constructor, Display, Select, LeftButtonPressed, LeftButtonReleased, destructor

Files used: screen.hpp and screen.cpp

Class: *TapeCounter*

Description: This class displays the instantaneous value of the array index used by the melody recorder. It behaves like the *tape counter* used in audio recorders. Acting on the recorder controls, the tape counter can be moved forward or backwards.

Parent class: *Icon*

Child classes: *ShadedBox*

Member functions: constructor, Display, Update, destructor

Files used: counter.hpp and counter.cpp

See also: *Keyboard, PianoKeyboard, Recorder, Melody*

Class: *SetupPopup*

Description: This is the implementation of the popup window that appears when you click on the *Setup* button on page *Recorder* of the demo program. It shows how to use the popup machinery of the base class to create derived popup windows.

Parent class: *PopupWindow*

Child classes: *ToneLevelPot, HorizontalSelector, BistablePushButton*

Member functions: constructor, Display, destructor

Files used: setup.hpp and setup.cpp

See also: *PopupWindow*

Class: *ToneButton*

Description: This class implements the music buttons shown on page *Games* of the demo program. It demonstrates techniques for deriving classes, adding new characteristics to preexistent ones.

Parent class: *MonostablePushButton*

Child classes: None

Member functions: constructor, LeftButtonPressed, LeftButtonReleased

Files used: tone.hpp and tone.cpp

Class: *TopLevel*

Description: This is the class containing the GUI's event loop, which should maintain control of the system at all times. Individual icons should not contain their own event loops because any delays occurring in them may disrupt normal display animation.

Parent class: None

Child classes: None

Member functions: constructor

Class: *Vat*

Description: This class implements a rectangular-looking water tank that constantly fills and empties itself with a colored fluid. It illustrates some of the features of animation.

Parent class: *Icon*

Child classes: *Box*

Member functions: constructor, DecreaseLevel, IncreaseLevel, Level, Display, Update, destructor

Files used: vat.hpp and vat.cpp

Class: *VatPage*

Description: This application page puts together three *Vat* objects. It is shown on page *Tanks* of the demo program.

Parent class: *Page*

Child classes: *Vat*

Member functions: constructor, Display, destructor

Files used: vatpage.hpp and vatpage.cpp

B

Using the DEMO Program

Running the DEMO Program

The files distributed with the system include the source files, header files, and executable programs. The demo program has the following versions:

bdemo.exe   compiled with Borland Turbo C++
zdemo.exe   compiled with Zortech C++

Both versions of the demo behave similarly. Version 1.0 of Turbo C++ was used for file *bdemo.exe*, and version 2.0 of Zortech C++ was used for file *zdemo.exe*. No library files will be found on the companion disk, because these are available from the compiler manufacturers.

The files available on the disk can be compiled with any C++ compiler compatible with AT&T release 2. The only exceptions are the *Graphics* and *Events* classes, which are compiler and machine dependent.

To run the demo program, you must have a PC or compatible computer with a Microsoft compatible mouse and EGA/VGA display adaptor. Log onto the companion diskette and type *bdemo* or *zdemo* at the DOS command level. To exit the program, click the right mouse button anywhere on the screen. Use the left mouse button to select icons or to act on them.

Installing Files from the Companion Disk

The companion disk has files for all the code described in this book, but you need to go through a simple installation procedure before you can use these files. The disk contains a single file, called code.exe, that is a self-extracting archived file. You need to create a directory to put all the book files in, then extract the archived files, by following these steps:

1. Create a directory on your hard disk called `\demo`. This directory will contain all the `*.cpp` and `*.hpp` files, plus the `*.obj` files compiled with the Zortech compiler.

2. Create a second directory called `\demo\tc`, to store the `*.obj` files generated by Turbo C++.

3. Change to directory `\demo`.

4. Copy the file `code.exe` on the companion disk into directory `\demo`.

5. Type the command code, to extract all the archived book files from `code.exe` and store them in directory `\demo`.

What you do next depends on which compiler you are going to use.

Using Turbo C++

Change to the *\demo* directory and insert the line

```
#define BORLAND TRUE
```

into the file *constant.hpp* using a word processor. Remove the ZORTECH macro if it is present. Type

```
TC
```

to start Turbo C++. To do this, you will need all the Turbo C++ directories in the DOS path setting. The files *bdemo.prj* and *bdemo.dsk* are automatically selected as the default project files. Press *Control-F9* to build the project and the *bdemo* program will be made. All the Turbo C++ *.obj* files will be saved in the directory *\demo\tc* so that they don't get mixed up with the *.obj* files generated by the Zortech compiler (which are saved in directory *\demo*).

Using Zortech C++

The Zortech system uses the MAKE program. This is supplied by Zortech with their compiler package. It requires two files to build the complete project: the MAKE command file and the linker command file. These are available on the companion disk under the filenames

makefile	MAKE command file
files.lnk	linker command file

Edit the file *constant.hpp* and insert the line

```
#define ZORTECH TRUE
```

Remove the BORLAND macro if it is present. Make sure the Zortech subdirectories are included in the DOS path setting. Type the command

```
\zortech\bin\make
```

at the DOS command prompt, and all files with be compiled and linked automatically, using the MEDIUM memory model. The MAKE program automatically saves the **.obj* files in the directory *\demo*. If you save your Zortech binary files under a different directory, you obviously must make the necessary adjustments. For convenience, the files *makefile* and *files.lnk* are listed here.

Listing B.1. The MAKE command file `makefile`.

```
zdemo:      applic.obj      \
            ball.obj        \
            box.obj         \
            clock.obj       \
            clocks.obj      \
            config.obj      \
            counter.obj     \
            database.obj    \
            delay.obj       \
            demo.obj        \
            descrip.obj     \
            die.obj         \
            events.obj      \
            games.obj       \
            icon.obj        \
            keyboard.obj    \
            legend.obj      \
            listmgr.obj     \
            lotto.obj       \
            melody.obj      \
```

Listing B.1 Continues

Listing B.1 Continued

```
                mouse.obj       \
                page.obj        \
                pagesel.obj     \
                piano.obj       \
                pianopg.obj     \
                pingpong.obj    \
                popup.obj       \
                pot.obj         \
                pushbut.obj     \
                random.obj      \
                recorder.obj    \
                screen.obj      \
                selector.obj    \
                setup.obj       \
                tone.obj        \
                top.obj         \
                vat.obj         \
                vatpage.obj     \
                zgraphics.obj


           blink @files.lnk

   applic.obj:      applic.cpp
                    ztc -c -mM -s applic.cpp

   ball.obj:        ball.cpp ball.hpp
                    ztc -c -mM -s ball.cpp

   box.obj:         box.cpp box.hpp
                    ztc -c -mM -s box.cpp

   clock.obj:       clock.cpp clock.hpp
                    ztc -c -mM -s clock.cpp

   clocks.obj:      clocks.cpp clocks.hpp
                    ztc -c -mM -s clocks.cpp

   config.obj:      config.cpp config.hpp database.hpp
                    ztc -c -mM -s config.cpp

   counter.obj:     counter.cpp counter.hpp
                    ztc -c -mM -s counter.cpp

   database.obj:    database.cpp database.hpp
                    ztc -c -mM -s database.cpp

   delay.obj:       delay.cpp delay.hpp
                    ztc -c -mM -s delay.cpp

   demo.obj:        demo.cpp
                    ztc -c -mM -s demo.cpp
```

```
descrip.obj:        descrip.cpp descrip.hpp limit.hpp
                    ztc -c -mM -s descrip.cpp

die.obj:            die.cpp die.hpp
                    ztc -c -mM -s die.cpp

events.obj:         events.cpp events.hpp limit.hpp
                    ztc -c -mM -s events.cpp

games.obj:          games.cpp games.hpp
                    ztc -c -mM -s games.cpp

icon.obj:           icon.cpp icon.hpp
                    ztc -c -mM -s icon.cpp

keyboard.obj:       keyboard.cpp keyboard.hpp
                    ztc -c -mM -s keyboard.cpp

legend.obj:         legend.cpp legend.hpp
                    ztc -c -mM -s legend.cpp

listmgr.obj:        listmgr.cpp listmgr.hpp
                    ztc -c -mM -s listmgr.cpp

lotto.obj:          lotto.cpp lotto.hpp
                    ztc -c -mM -s lotto.cpp

melody.obj:         melody.cpp melody.hpp
                    ztc -c -mM -s melody.cpp

mouse.obj:          mouse.cpp mouse.hpp
                    ztc -c -mM -s mouse.cpp

page.obj:           page.cpp page.hpp limit.hpp
                    ztc -c -mM -s page.cpp

pagesel.obj:        pagesel.cpp pagesel.hpp
                    ztc -c -mM -s pagesel.cpp

piano.obj:          piano.cpp piano.hpp
                    ztc -c -mM -s piano.cpp

pianopg.obj:        pianopg.cpp pianopg.hpp
                    ztc -c -mM -s pianopg.cpp

pingpong.obj:       pingpong.cpp pingpong.hpp
                    ztc -c -mM -s pingpong.cpp

popup.obj:          popup.cpp popup.hpp
                    ztc -c -mM -s popup.cpp
```

Listing B.1 Continues

Listing B.1 Continued

```
pot.obj:          pot.cpp pot.hpp
                  ztc -c -mM -s pot.cpp

pushbut.obj:      pushbut.cpp pushbut.hpp limit.hpp
                  ztc -c -mM -s pushbut.cpp

random.obj:       random.cpp random.hpp
                  ztc -c -mM -s random.cpp

recorder.obj:     recorder.cpp recorder.hpp
                  ztc -c -mM -s recorder.cpp

screen.obj:       screen.cpp screen.hpp
                  ztc -c -mM -s screen.cpp

selector.obj:     selector.cpp selector.hpp
                  ztc -c -mM -s selector.cpp

setup.obj:        setup.cpp setup.hpp database.hpp
                  ztc -c -mM -s setup.cpp

tone.obj:         tone.cpp tone.hpp
                  ztc -c -mM -s tone.cpp

top.obj:          top.cpp top.hpp
                  ztc -c -mM -s top.cpp

vat.obj:          vat.cpp vat.hpp
                  ztc -c -mM -s vat.cpp

vatpage.obj:      vatpage.cpp vatpage.hpp
                  ztc -c -mM -s vatpage.cpp

zgraphics.obj: zgraphics.cpp zgraphics.hpp
limit.hpp
                  ztc -c -mM -s zgraphics.cpp
```

Listing B.2. The linker command file `files.lnk`.

```
applic.obj+
ball.obj+
box.obj+
clock.obj+
clocks.obj+
config.obj+
counter.obj+
database.obj+
delay.obj+
demo.obj+
descrip.obj+
```

```
die.obj+
events.obj+
games.obj+
icon.obj+
keyboard.obj+
legend.obj+
listmgr.obj+
lotto.obj+
melody.obj+
mouse.obj+
page.obj+
pagesel.obj+
piano.obj+
pianopg.obj+
pingpong.obj+
popup.obj+
pot.obj+
pushbut.obj+
random.obj+
recorder.obj+
screen.obj+
selector.obj+
setup.obj+
tone.obj+
top.obj+
vat.obj+
vatpage.obj+
zgraphics.obj
zdemo, zdemo, \zortech\lib\fg.lib +
\zortech\lib\fgm.lib
```

Bibliography

Articles

A Guide to Graphical User Interfaces, *BYTE* magazine cover story, vol. 14 no. 7.

Bar-David, Tsvi. Designing and implementing a text editor using OOP, parts 1, 2, 3; *The C Users Journal*, vol 8 no. 1, 3, 5.

Porter, Kent. Mouse mysteries, parts 1-2, *Turbo Technix*, vol. 1 numbers 4, 5.

Ruddell, K. Write faster graphics programs by using offscreen bitmap manipulation, *Microsoft Systems Journal*, vol. 4 no. 5.

Stroustrup, B. Object oriented programming, a better C?, *BYTE* magazine, vol. 14 no. 3.

The NewWave Environment, *Hewlett-Packard Journal*, entire issue, vol. 40 no 4.

Thomson, T. and N. Baron. The NeXT Computer, *BYTE* magazine, vol. 13 no. 12.

Valdes, R. A Virtual Toolkit for Windows and the Mac, *BYTE* magazine, vol. 14 no. 3.

Books

Cox, Brad J.: *Object Oriented Programming*, Addison-Wesley, Reading, MA 1987, ISBN 0-201-10393-1.

Meyer, Bertrand: *Object Oriented Software Construction*, Prentice Hall, Englewood Cliffs, NJ 1988, ISBN 0-13-629049-3.

Microsoft Corp.: *Microsoft Mouse Programmer's Reference*, Microsoft Press, Redmond, WA 1989, ISBN 1-55615-191-8.

Petzold, Charles: *Programming Windows*, Microsoft Press, Redmond, WA 1988, ISBN 0-914845-91-8.

Pohl, Ira: *C++ for C Programmers*, Benjamin Cummings Co. Inc., Menlo Park, CA 1989, ISBN 0-8053-0910-1.

Stevens, Al: *Extending Turbo C Professional*, MIS:Press, Portland, OR 1989, ISBN 1-55828-013-8.

Stevens, Roger T.: *Graphics Programming in C*, M&T Books, Redwood City, CA 1989, ISBN 1-55851-018-4.

Stroustrup, Bjarne: *The C++ Programming Language*, Addison-Wesley, Reading, MA 1987, ISBN 0-201-12078-X.

Index

C

D

E

G

H

I

K

Sams—Covering The Latest In Computer And Technical Topics!

Audio

Audio Production Techniques for Video $29.95
Audio Systems Design and Installation $59.95
Audio Technology Fundamentals $24.95
Compact Disc Troubleshooting and Repair $24.95
Handbook for Sound Engineers:
   The New Audio Cyclopedia $79.95
Introduction to Professional Recording Techniques $29.95
Modern Recording Techniques, 3rd Ed. $29.95
Principles of Digital Audio, 2nd Ed. $29.95
Sound Recording Handbook $49.95
Sound System Engineering, 2nd Ed. $49.95

Electricity/Electronics

Basic AC Circuits $29.95
Electricity 1, Revised 2nd Ed. $14.95
Electricity 1-7, Revised 2nd Ed. $49.95
Electricity 2, Revised 2nd Ed. $14.95
Electricity 3, Revised 2nd Ed. $14.95
Electricity 4, Revised 2nd Ed. $14.95
Electricity 5, Revised 2nd Ed. $14.95
Electricity 6, Revised 2nd Ed. $14.95
Electricity 7, Revised 2nd Ed. $14.95
Electronics 1-7, Revised 2nd Ed. $49.95

Electronics Technical

Active-Filter Cookbook $19.95
Camcorder Survival Guide . . . .$ 9.95
CMOS Cookbook, 2nd Ed. $24.95
Design of OP-AMP Circuits with Experiments . . .$19.95
Design of Phase-Locked Loop Circuits
   with Experiments $19.95
Electrical Test Equipment $19.95
Electrical Wiring $19.95
How to Read Schematics, 4th Ed. $19.95
IC Op-Amp Cookbook, 3rd Ed. $24.95
IC Timer Cookbook, 2nd Ed. $19.95
IC User's Casebook $19.95
Radio Handbook, 23rd Ed. $39.95
Radio Operator's License Q&A Manual, 11th Ed. . .$24.95
RF Circuit Design $24.95
Transformers and Motors $24.95
TTL Cookbook $19.95
Undergrounding Electric Lines $14.95
Understanding Telephone Electronics, 2nd Ed. . .$19.95
VCR Troubleshooting & Repair Guide $19.95
Video Scrambling & Descrambling
   for Satellite & Cable TV $19.95

Games

Beyond the Nintendo Masters . . . .$ 9.95
Mastering Nintendo Video Games II . . . .$ 9.95
Tricks of the Nintendo Masters . . . .$ 9.95
VideoGames & Computer Entertainment
   Complete Guide to Nintendo Video Games . .$ 9.50
Winner's Guide to Nintendo Game Boy . . . . . .$ 9.95
Winner's Guide to Sega Genesis . . . .$ 9.95

Hardware/Technical

Hard Disk Power with the Jamsa Disk Utilities . .$39.95
IBM PC Advanced Troubleshooting & Repair . . .$24.95
IBM Personal Computer
   Troubleshooting & Repair $24.95
IBM Personal Computer Upgrade Guide $24.95
Microcomputer Troubleshooting & Repair $24.95
Understanding Communications Systems, 2nd Ed. $19.95
Understanding Data Communications, 2nd Ed. . .$19.95
Understanding FAX and Electronic Mail $19.95
Understanding Fiber Optics $19.95

IBM: Business

Best Book of Microsoft Works for the PC, 2nd Ed. $24.95
Best Book of PFS: First Choice $24.95
Best Book of Professional Write and File $22.95
First Book of Fastback Plus $16.95
First Book of Norton Utilities $16.95
First Book of Personal Computing $16.95
First Book of PROCOMM PLUS $16.95

IBM: Database

Best Book of Paradox 3 . . . .$27.95
dBASE III Plus Programmer's Reference Guide . .$24.95
dBASE IV Programmer's Reference Guide $24.95
First Book of Paradox 3 . . . .$16.95
Mastering ORACLE
   Featuring ORACLE's SQL Standard $24.95

IBM: Graphics/Desktop Publishing

Best Book of Autodesk Animator $29.95
Best Book of Harvard Graphics $24.95
First Book of DrawPerfect $16.95
First Book of Harvard Graphics $16.95
First Book of PC Paintbrush $16.95
First Book of PFS: First Publisher $16.95

IBM: Spreadsheets/Financial

Best Book of Lotus 1-2-3 Release 3.1 . . . . . .$27.95
Best Book of Lotus 1-2-3, Release 2.2, 3rd Ed. .$26.95
Best Book of Peachtree Complete III $24.95
First Book of Lotus 1-2-3, Release 2.2 . . . . .$16.95
First Book of Lotus 1-2-3/G $16.95
First Book of Microsoft Excel for the PC $16.95
Lotus 1-2-3: Step-by-Step $24.95

IBM: Word Processing

Best Book of Microsoft Word 5 . . . .$24.95
Best Book of Microsoft Word for Windows $24.95
Best Book of WordPerfect 5.1 . . . .$26.95
Best Book of WordPerfect Version 5.0 . . . . . .$24.95
First Book of PC Write $16.95
First Book of WordPerfect 5.1 . . . .$16.95
WordPerfect 5.1: Step-by-Step $24.95

Macintosh/Apple

Best Book of AppleWorks $24.95
Best Book of MacWrite II $24.95
Best Book of Microsoft Word for the Macintosh . .$24.95
Macintosh Printer Secrets $34.95
Macintosh Repair & Upgrade Secrets $34.95
Macintosh Revealed, Expanding the Toolbox,
   Vol. 4 . . . .$29.95
Macintosh Revealed, Mastering the Toolbox,
   Vol. 3 . . . .$29.95
Macintosh Revealed, Programming with the Toolbox,
   Vol. 2, 2nd Ed. $29.95
Macintosh Revealed, Unlocking the Toolbox,
   Vol. 1, 2nd Ed. $29.95
Using ORACLE with HyperCard $24.95

Operating Systems/Networking

Best Book of DESQview $24.95
Best Book of DOS $24.95
Best Book of Microsoft Windows 3 . . . .$24.95
Business Guide to Local Area Networks $24.95
Exploring the UNIX System, 2nd Ed. $29.95
First Book of DeskMate $16.95
First Book of Microsoft QuickPascal $16.95
First Book of MS-DOS $16.95
First Book of UNIX $16.95
Interfacing to the IBM Personal Computer,
   2nd Ed. $24.95
Mastering NetWare $29.95
The Waite Group's Discovering MS-DOS $19.95
The Waite Group's Inside XENIX $29.95
The Waite Group's MS-DOS Bible, 3rd Ed. $24.95
The Waite Group's MS-DOS Developer's Guide,
   2nd Ed. $29.95
The Waite Group's Tricks of the MS-DOS Masters,
   2nd Ed. $29.95
The Waite Group's Tricks of the UNIX Masters $29.95
The Waite Group's Understanding MS-DOS,
   2nd Ed. $19.95
The Waite Group's UNIX Primer Plus, 2nd Ed. . .$29.95
The Waite Group's UNIX System V Bible $29.95
The Waite Group's UNIX System V Primer,
   Revised Ed. $29.95
Understanding Local Area Networks, 2nd Ed. . . .$24.95

Understanding NetWare $24.95
UNIX Applications Programming:
   Mastering the Shell $29.95
UNIX Networking $29.95
UNIX Shell Programming, Revised Ed. $29.95
UNIX System Administration $29.95
UNIX System Security $34.95
UNIX Text Processing $29.95
UNIX: Step-by-Step $29.95

Professional/Reference

Data Communications, Networks, and Systems . .$39.95
Gallium Arsenide Technology, Volume II $69.95
Handbook of Computer-Communications Standards,
   Vol. 1, 2nd Ed. $39.95
Handbook of Computer-Communications Standards,
   Vol. 2, 2nd Ed. $39.95
Handbook of Computer-Communications Standards,
   Vol. 3, 2nd Ed. $39.95
Handbook of Electronics Tables and Formulas,
   6th Ed. $24.95
ISDN, DECnet, and SNA Communications $44.95
Modern Dictionary of Electronics, 6th Ed. $39.95
Programmable Logic Designer's Guide $29.95
Reference Data for Engineers: Radio, Electronics,
   Computer, and Communications, 7th Ed. . . .$99.95
Surface-Mount Technology for PC Board Design .$49.95
World Satellite Almanac, 2nd Ed. $39.95

Programming

Advanced C: Tips and Techniques $29.95
C Programmer's Guide to NetBIOS $29.95
C Programmer's Guide to Serial Communications $29.95
Commodore 64 Programmer's Reference Guide .$19.95
DOS Batch File Power $39.95
First Book of GW-BASIC $16.95
How to Write Macintosh Software, 2nd Ed. $29.95
Mastering Turbo Assembler $29.95
Mastering Turbo Debugger $29.95
Mastering Turbo Pascal 5.5, 3rd Ed. $29.95
Microsoft QuickBASIC Programmer's Reference $29.95
Programming in ANSI C $29.95
Programming in C, Revised Ed. $29.95
QuickC Programming $29.95
The Waite Group's BASIC Programming
   Primer, 2nd Ed. $24.95
The Waite Group's C Programming
   Using Turbo C++ $29.95
The Waite Group's C++ Programming $24.95
The Waite Group's C: Step-by-Step $29.95
The Waite Group's GW-BASIC Primer Plus $24.95
The Waite Group's Microsoft C Bible, 2nd Ed. . .$29.95
The Waite Group's Microsoft C Programming
   for the PC, 2nd Ed. $29.95
The Waite Group's Microsoft Macro
   Assembler Bible $29.95
The Waite Group's New C Primer Plus $29.95
The Waite Group's QuickC Bible $29.95
The Waite Group's Turbo Assembler Bible $29.95
The Waite Group's Turbo C Bible $29.95
The Waite Group's Turbo C Programming
   for the PC, Revised Ed. $29.95
The Waite Group's TWG Turbo C++Bible $29.95
X Window System Programming $29.95

For More Information, Call Toll Free

1-800-257-5755

*All prices are subject to change without notice.
Non-U.S. prices may be higher. Printed in the U.S.A.*

If your computer uses 3 1/2-inch disks . . .

Although most personal computers use 5 1/4-inch disks to store information, some newer computers are switching to 3 1/2-inch disks for information storage. If your computer uses 3 1/2-inch disks, you can return this form to SAMS to obtain a 3 1/2-inch disk to use with this book. Simply fill out the remainder of this form, and mail to:

GUI with Turbo C++
Disk Exchange
SAMS
11711 N. College Ave., Suite 140
Carmel, IN 46032

We will then send you, free of charge, the 3 1/2-inch version of the book software.

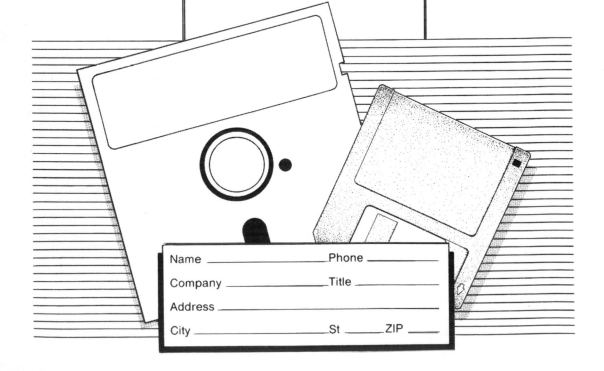

Name _____ Phone _____

Company _____ Title _____

Address _____

City _____ St _____ ZIP _____